SANDRA GORDON STOLTZ

THE
FOOD FIX

A Recovery Guide
for Destructive Eaters

Foreword by Harvey M. Ross, M.D.

Illustrations by Jackie Urbanovic

PRENTICE HALL PRESS
New York London Toronto Sydney Tokyo

Published in 1986 by Prentice Hall Press
A Division of Simon & Schuster, Inc.
Gulf + Western Building
One Gulf + Western Plaza
New York, NY 10023

Originally published by Prentice-Hall, Inc.

PRENTICE HALL PRESS is a trademark of Simon & Schuster, Inc.

Library of Congress Cataloging-in-Publication Data

Stolz, Sandra Gordon.
The food fix.

Includes index.
1. Nutritionally induced diseases—Prevention.
2. Food habits. 3. Behavior modification. I. Title.
RC622.S78   1983   616.3'908   83-9590
ISBN 0-13-323105-4 (pbk.)

Manufactured in the United States of America

13   12   11   10   9   8   7   6

Contents

FOODAHOLISM AND PHYSICAL ADDICTION

THE FOODAHOLIC WAY OF LIFE

GETTING WELL: CHANGING LIFESTYLES

PREVENTION IS THE BEST MEDICINE

Foreword

Estimates of the prevalance of hypoglycemia in the adult population range from 10 percent to 50 percent and the occurrence of food sensitivities probably exceeds that of hypoglycemia. If you then include the percentage of those who are affected by Foodaholism, there is probably no one who would not be touched significantly by paying attention to the content of the following pages of *The Food Fix.*

As a practicing physician who has spent a great deal of time treating hypoglycemia and food sensitivities, it is obvious to me that these are far from "fad" conditions. Rather they are serious problems which significantly affect the health and life of large segments of the population. The symptoms may be devastating. Hypoglycemia usually results in excessive fatigue, depression in those who frequently have nothing to be depressed about, irritability such that relating to others becomes an almost impossible task, anxiety which may proceed to phobias, and usually fuzziness in thinking. Unfortunately hypoglycemia usually remains undiagnosed for a few years, resulting in psychological problems such as loss of self-esteem and feelings of worthlessness.

The effects of food sensitivities are even more general than the effects of hypoglycemia. Any food to which the person is sensitive may affect any system or organ of the body. The results of food sensitivities may range from the mildest of skin irritability to severe disorders of the nervous system which lead to mood changes, behavioral disorders, and perceptual distortions resembling schizophrenia.

Other eating disorders such as bulimia, anorexia, and obesity have captured the interest of the medical profession, yet food sensitivities and hypoglycemia have remained on the fringes of established medicine. Considering the enormity of the problem, the lack of attention given by the medical profession is more than unfortunate and has resulted in much more suffering than is necessary. The general population is beginning to recognize the weaknesses as well as the strengths of the medical profession and appreciate that health care begins with the individual and not in the doctor's office.

The Food Fix joins in the growing realization that one is responsible for one's own health. Instead of blaming others the message is clearly, "It's your health. You take charge." But in order to take charge we must have some basic information telling us how to recognize a problem and then what to do about it. In sharing with us her valuable personal and professional experiences in the realms of the physical, nutritional, and psychological aspects of the Foodaholic, Sandra Gordon Stoltz provides us with basic information necessary for one to take charge of one's own Foodaholic problem.

Harvey M. Ross, M.D.
President, The International College of Applied Nutrition
President, The Academy of Orthomolecular Psychiatry

Acknowledgments

I am grateful and awed that the following talented people were willing to contribute their support and expertise to me and to this book. I am indebted to:

Timothy Chadsey, for work on the preliminary manuscript, a literature survey, and the title.

Jackie Urbanovic for her delightful, sensitive, and humorous cartoons.

Dr. Harvey M. Ross, whose work and writings on orthomolecular nutrition partially provide the orientation of Part II, and for agreeing to write the foreword.

Kate Thomson for the research and much of the writing in the Food Allergies and Anorexia/Bulimia chapters, and for typing the final manuscript.

Pamela Levin Landheer for evaluation and enrichment of the developmental material in the How NOT to Raise a Foodaholic chapter.

Deane Gradous for technical editing with an emotional investment, dedication, and thoroughness that were an inspiration to me.

Ann King and Kathleen Ann Michels for technical editing.

Judith Barnitt, Helen Gilbert, Deane Gradous, Robert Griswold, Ann King, Kathleen Ann Michels, and Kate Thomson for reviewing and evaluating the manuscript.

Robert Griswold and Karen West for their strong encouragement during the difficult early phases.

Priscilla Clayton and Kate Thomson for securing copyright permissions.

Ronelle Ewing for editing, rewriting, and preparing of the final manuscript for publication.

WITH CAREFUL PLANNING AND CONCENTRATED
EATING I CAN EXCHANGE GLOOM AND
BOREDOM FOR BLISSFUL NUMBNESS.

Why This Book?

To a drug user, a "fix" is an injection of heroin or other narcotic. I have titled this book *The Food Fix,* because I believe that, for some of us, food is our drug of choice. We use—and abuse—food for many of the same reasons that other people use and abuse narcotics or alcohol: to punish ourselves, to reward ourselves, to escape from problems, to demonstrate feelings of helplessness and hopelessness. We use food to "fix" ourselves and our lives and to mend our wounded feelings. We expect eating to change things for the better. And it may, for a while. Ultimately, though, its effects are negative.

Given the striking similarities between alcoholism and food abuse, I have come to refer to people with eating disorders as Foodaholics. I believe that Foodaholism—just as drug and alcohol abuse—should be classified and treated as a disorder or disease, rather than a moral weakness or a character defect.

The primary symptom of Foodaholism is destructive eating—consumption of the kinds and quantities of food which are harmful to our bodies, our minds, our emotions, and our relationships. Eating destructively can diminish our energy, emotional stability, and mental clarity. It can impair our health and shorten our lives.

Foodaholism, like alcoholism, is a family disease. It also has a social basis. We live in a Foodaholic society.

The onset of this disease may be sudden or gradual. Its cause may be mild or acute, episodic or chronic. If I over-indulge and feel somewhat ill or under par only during the time between Thanksgiving and New Year's, I'm still a Foodaholic. In this case, my behavior is similar to that of an alcoholic who goes on a bender for two weeks every six months.

Professional help may be necessary for recovery from this disease. The treatment may be short-term or long-term, depending on the individual. Prognosis for recovery from Foodaholism has, until recently, been poor. Remissions are frequent, but while they are sometimes permanent and real, more often they are temporary and artificially induced by a form of deprivation we euphemistically call "dieting."

Dieting produces only temporary remission in Foodaholics because it focuses simply on the removal of symptoms—leading to a decrease in body size or the amount of food consumed. This approach is akin to treating a broken bone with a pain pill. We don't expect to regain our mobility until the bone has been properly reset and has healed. Yet we Foodaholics repeatedly attempt to lose weight or alter our intake of food and meet with limited success, because we haven't treated the other components of our eating disorder.

Believing that we are personally helpless or hopeless is part of our Foodaholic pattern. Typically, we have an assortment of such self-defeating beliefs which comprise our Foodaholic Thought Disorder. The hopeless monologue in our heads sounds something like this:

"Oh, I'll try this diet too, but it won't work for long. They never do."

"Sure I'm thin now, but just wait. I always gain it back."

"No matter how healthy I eat, I binge every weekend. I have ever since I was a child."

"First comes the stuffing down of everything in sight and then comes the vomiting." (The internal monologue of the bulimic.)

We Foodaholics somehow feel that we are helpless in overcoming our problem. Food abuse, like our weight, lifestyle, and activity are perceived as "just happening" to us—like being rained upon or missing a bus that left early. Some of us manage to convince ourselves that our mothers —often persuasive purveyors of sweets—determine what we eat. Some of us manage to keep our homes always fully stocked with junk foods to fuel the growth and meet the demands of family teenagers. Some of us manage to shop for a month's supply of high-calorie, non-nutritional snacks for grandpa's weekend visit because, after all, he's entitled to eat whatever he wants at this time in his life. When we give people and circumstances outside ourselves power to control our lives and our eating behavior, is it any wonder we also look outside ourselves for a solution, the cure to make us healthier and happier?

But the real key to recovery lies in understanding this simple concept: Our Foodaholism is a choice and we *do* have all the power we need to get well, if we choose to exercise that power.

The kind of power essential to recover from Foodaholism is our willingness and ability to take or regain responsibility for our own lives, it is not "willpower." Contrary to what most people think, *recovery from Foodaholism does not start with a diet or with the decision to go on a diet.* In fact, dieting often contributes more to the problem than to the solution. We eat destructively because of negative feelings about our bodies, our ability to love and be loved, or our ability to control our own lives. Then, in order to gain some control of the destructive eating, we turn to other negative concepts like dieting and weight loss.

Dieting is a negative concept when we use it negatively, which we usually do. We want to muster our willpower and diet successfully for as long as it takes us to reach our ideal weight or build a better body. We fuel our willpower by hounding ourselves about our inadequacies, physical and otherwise, berating ourselves for our weakness, and fanning our self-hatred.

RECOVERING FROM FOODAHOLISM

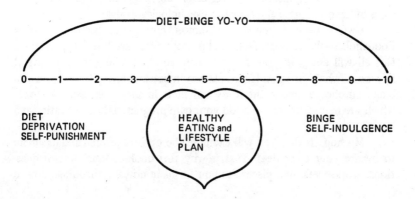

3

Dieting is a negative concept: a program of *not* eating—*not* eating too many calories, *not* eating fattening foods, *not* eating between-meal snacks, *not* eating favorite foods. Furthermore, we may actually be *seeking* self-punishment or deprivation by inflicting a diet upon ourselves.

Dieting is a negative concept because it involves personal loss. It means giving up food. It means giving up pounds and body size. For some of us, a change in body image has profound and frightening implications which need to be brought into awareness and dealt with *before* we make these changes.

Because dieting, as we know it, is so closely tied to negative thoughts and ideas, we probably need to abandon it as a concept in order to recover from Foodaholism.

If you are reading this book searching for a miracle diet or a magic plan that will enable you to shed weight instantly, you will be sorely disappointed. There is no guaranteed weight loss in this treatment program. Furthermore, I discourage rapid weight loss. If you believe that only a program of deprivation will work for you, if you want to read messages such as: "Get on the stick," "Control yourself," "Shape up," "Do it right," you won't find them here. If you want to suffer, close the book, give it to a friend or return it to the store, and enlist one of your critical friends or family to scold you into action.

If, however, you are ready to concentrate on *gains*, if you are ready to develop a positive program of self-care, bodily awareness, and healthy eating to replace your destructive patterns of using food to abuse your body, you've come to the right place.

In order to facilitate your designing a positive program for yourself, I will be exploring the emotional or psychological factors common to people with eating disorders. I will offer some suggestions for alternative ways of handling these emotional or psychological issues.

I will share with you some common traits I have discovered among Foodaholics—the feelings, facts, and processes that are true for most of us. Not all will apply to you. I don't want you to swallow the contents of this book whole or to stuff them down indiscriminately. I hope you will pick and choose among the ideas and facts in the book, using the ones which are helpful to you to build your own program of healthy eating and living.

My hope is that you will examine the options offered and use them to inspire your own ideas. That is why this book contains lots of questions, worksheets, and places for you to make notes. I encourage you to try new behaviors, to experiment with a number of different ways of dealing with your eating and your life, to keep only those techniques and ideas that work for you, and to discard the rest. What you'll be doing is developing a program that meets your needs and is uniquely your own. The guidelines to keep in mind as you design a personalized program are: (1) Does it work well for me? (2) Is it healthy for me physically and emotionally, both on a short-term basis and in the long run? (3) Does it cause no harm to others?

I invite you to answer the questions, think, plan, fill in the worksheets, and then "work your program" to the best of your ability. As you work the program, your behavior patterns will come into sharp focus, giving you opportunities to confront the excuses and "cons" you offer yourself and others in order to perpetuate your destructive eating. Continuing your work will enable you to become aware of the needs and feelings underlying your eating problems, and to acquaint yourself with the healthy alternatives that exist for meeting your needs and dealing with your feelings.

The patterns, perceptions, and prescriptions described in this book originate in the Foodaholic groups I have led since 1975. Many former and current group members are recovering from foodaholism. Whereas I used to believe that recovery from Foodaholism was a lifelong process, as with chemical dependency, I now think cure is achievable for some people. Most of us certainly enjoy life more fully now and we really accept and appreciate ourselves. Some of us are noticing a beneficial side effect— losing weight gradually and keeping it off without hassling ourselves or feeling punished, because our need for food and our interest in food have diminished.

We have learned that after eating nutritious or "clean" foods we feel good and that after eating junk food* we feel bad. We begin to *prefer* healthier foods because we are more in tune with our bodies and have a heightened awareness of our physical response to different substances. We have learned to value ourselves and our bodies, so we seek to maintain the

---

*The term "junk food" in this book refers to products that are made "unnatural" through processes such as overrefining, manufacturing, or sweetening. Most of these foods are carbohydrates containing one or more forms of sugar, added fats, and/or white flour. They provide many calories and little nutrition.

Fruits, vegetables (including potatoes), whole grains and legumes are natural or complex carbohydrates. Other healthy foods include snacks such as popcorn, nuts, seeds, and dried or fresh fruit.

enhanced energy, calmness, and intellectual clarity that we experience when we maintain a healthy perspective on eating rather than a preoccupation with it. Without that preoccupation, we feel light and free. It is like getting a load off our shoulders or a "monkey off our back."

We have learned how to give ourselves real rewards or treats, instead of *mis*treating ourselves with junk food or sweets. We have built new lives for ourselves that offer natural highs instead of the temporary and artificial good feelings we used to seek from food. We acknowledge that we are still addictive personalities and may always be. Now, however, we have some positive addictions that include the natural and joyful feeling of good health.

Your recovery depends on you. You might latch onto one "on-target golden nugget" from the options in this treatment program and use it to dramatically turn your life around. Or, you might "work the program" steadily and slowly, improving month by month and year by year. Whether your recovery is relatively fast or a more gradual process is not important. What is important is that you heal yourself at your own rate, with patience, and without self-punishment, self-criticism, and perfectionism.

This book is meant to be a healing one, a nurturing, forgiving, and very human one. I hope it will be contagious and that you, too, will focus on healing, nurturing, and forgiving yourself, and allowing yourself to be very human.

TAKING
INVENTORY

1

The Destructive Eating Questionnaire and Scoring Index

The first step in designing your program of healthy eating is to assess the nature and scope of your food abuse. The process of putting a lifetime of destructive eating into perspective is not a simple one. But if you have a pencil, you can start right now by filling out the Destructive Eating Questionnaire[1] which follows.

The questionnaire will provide information about your eating patterns in three ways. First, honest answers to the questions in each category will heighten your awareness about specific ways in which you are or are not a Foodaholic. Second, compared to the Scoring Index designed by testing Foodaholics and non-Foodaholics your total score will graphically show you the extent of your Foodaholism. Third, the information, examples, and anecdotes included in the questionnaire itself will provide you with insights about the nature of Foodaholism.

A few tips on how to make the most of the questionnaire: Don't feel you need to take each question or example literally. Instead, use these questions and examples to jog your memory about related situations or statements that apply to your own experience. Think about your past as well as your present, even if it's tempting to dismiss many of the statements because you've been successfully controlling your food intake for a while. And, since the questionnaire is just the beginning of your program, you may want to jot down for future reference any thoughts or memories that occur to you while you're taking it.

Rate each statement on a scale of 4 to 0 as follows:

4   Usually
3   Frequently
2   Sometimes
1   Rarely
0   Never

FOODAHOLISM

1. The Food Fixation

4 3 2 1 0   Are you preoccupied with food and your next opportunity to eat?

4 3 2 1 0   Have you missed what someone was saying because you were thinking about food? Examples: lingering over the restaurant menu after others have made their choices and turned to conversation; losing your train of thought or another's words as you ogle some attractive food in a restaurant or store, at a party, or on TV.

4 3 2 1 0   At parties, does the buffet or food supply feel like a magnet to you? Examples: nibbling throughout the evening, holding court at the buffet with others who come and go; or resolving to be virtuous and spending your evening, and your energy, resisting the seductive pull of food.

4 3 2 1 0   Have you made mistakes at work because you're thinking of food?

4 3 2 1 0   Does staying in touch with food make it hard for people to get in touch with you? Examples: because of your trips to the office candy machine you are missing important phone calls or deadlines; grabbing a soft drink between classes makes you unavailable to people who want to talk to you

4 3 2 1 0   Have you encountered a potentially dangerous situation while driving because your attention was on eating?

Subtotal: _____

Many Foodaholics report that they think about food all the time. "What shall I eat next?" is our most frequently faced decision. Our preoccupation with food, the eating or not eating of it, is one factor that differentiates a Foodaholic from one who is not. This same preoccupation helps to differentiate an alcoholic from a social drinker.

2. The Food-Centered Lifestyle

4 3 2 1 0   Is what to serve your first decision when planning a party? Examples: working up the menu before deciding whom to invite; worrying about the presentation of the food rather than how well your guests will mix; providing specific foods, rather than activities, to please individual guests or the group.

4 3 2 1 0   Do you have friends who are *primarily* eating or dieting buddies?

4 3 2 1 0   Is eating out your chief form of entertainment?

4 3 2 1 0   Does your conversation focus on food, restaurants, recipes, or diets?

4 3 2 1 0   Are you disappointed when your companions are reluctant to go to your favorite restaurant?

4 3 2 1 0   Do you select and anticipate what you'll be eating before you arrive home, at a party, or at a restaurant when you've eaten within four hours and are not genuinely hungry?

Subtotal: _____

If you have a food-centered lifestyle, you probably choose to have several people in your life who share your intense interest in eating, dieting, or both. They are your equivalent of the alcoholic's drinking buddies. You also probably use dining out as a form of recreation to the exclusion of physical games or exercise, plays, concerts, movies, lectures, museums, or sporting events. For added awareness, notice what subjects people in your life bring up when they're trying to talk with you. Do they ask how the food was on your vacation or at the party you just attended? Do they ask about your newest restaurant "find"? Do they ask your opinion of a particular diet program?

3. The Fast Foodaholic

4 3 2 1 0   Do you eat quickly?

4 3 2 1 0   Do you wonder where your food went, because you do not remember finishing it?

11

4 3 2 1 0   Are you through eating before everyone else?

4 3 2 1 0   Do you eat your food without tasting it very much?

4 3 2 1 0   Do you find you've barely enjoyed your meal, snack, or binge?

Subtotal: _____

Some of us claim that eating is our chief joy in life or our only remaining vice. Yet the fast Foodaholic behaviors described certainly lessen our pleasure. As a result, we need more food to feel satisfied.

4. The Closet Foodaholic

4 3 2 1 0   Do you have some preference for eating alone?

4 3 2 1 0   Would you prefer not having others see what, how much, or how often you eat?

4 3 2 1 0   Do you eat sparingly with others, and consume more later?

4 3 2 1 0   Do you snack behind the scenes while you are helping, visiting, or preparing foods?

4 3 2 1 0   Do you eat in your car?

Subtotal: _____

It's typical of some Foodaholics to feel guilty, embarrassed, or ashamed about others knowing what we eat, what we want to eat, or how much we notice and enjoy food. We are very secretive.

5. The Food Fix-up

4 3 2 1 0   Do you use food as medicine?

4 3 2 1 0   Do you seek food when you have a problem to solve?

4 3 2 1 0   Do you have specific foods or quantities of food which you use to help you handle uncomfortable emotions? Example: eating a hot fudge sundae for lunch when you feel nervous about an important afternoon meeting.

4 3 2 1 0   Do you use food to fill the void inside you or in your life? Example: preparing cinnamon toast and hot chocolate, just like Mom did, on a Saturday night when you wish you were out on a date.

4 3 2 1 0   Do you eat to relieve tiredness or boredom or to keep yourself awake?

4 3 2 1 0   Do you eat to help you sleep?

4 3 2 1 0   Do you eat when you're not hungry, because you *might get hungry* if you don't?

Subtotal: _____

We Foodaholics want life to be calm, happy, and pleasant. When the reality of our lives doesn't match our expectations, we prefer the sedative effect of carbohydrates or large amounts of food rather than experiencing "forbidden" feelings: tension, anger, sadness, fear, boredom, loneliness, or even hunger! We often seek to comfort ourselves with the foods our parents offered us during childhood in lieu of reassuring hugs or words.

6. The Snack Thief

4 3 2 1 0   Do you hide food or sneak it? Examples: stashing goodies behind some big bowls or packages in the cupboard; keeping a candy bar in a drawer or the glove compartment of your car; hiding treats in a picnic hamper during the off season for picnics.

4 3 2 1 0   Have you lied about what or how much you've eaten? Examples: telling a family member who comments on the size of your dinner helpings that you've eaten little all day; raving about the marvelous salad bar you went to for lunch, failing to mention the garlic toast and dessert; reassuring your physician that you're much more careful these days, while visualizing the remainder of a box of chocolates in your desk.

4 3 2 1 0   Have you stolen food or money to buy it in order to support your habit? Examples: shaving off a tiny slice from a dessert being saved for someone else; grabbing more than your share ahead of time in the kitchen; when you're visiting, taking some attractive food that is not being served, and hoping it won't be missed.

4 3 2 1 0   Are you stingy or ungenerous with your food supply? Examples: tucking the last bit of the ice cream in the back of the freezer; keeping back half of the pan of brownies you made for the church bake sale; hiding a bag of chips in your office so you won't have to share it with co-workers.

4 3 2 1 0   Do you feel strong emotion toward someone who tampers with your food supply? Examples: feeling momentary anger or dislike for the friend who reaches for the last piece of pizza; resenting a friend who reminds you of your diet when you order dessert.

Subtotal: _____

You may have cringed somewhat at the questions in this section—the behaviors they describe are too much like those of drunks or junkies. But the fact is that food abuse, like alcohol and drug abuse, does have negative effects on our character. I was confronted with the scope of my Foodaholism when one of my old high school chums confided, years later: "You know, Sandra, for a while there, I really hated you. When your mom asked if you had anything to eat at the movie, you'd say, 'Annie had six candy bars, and I only had a bite of hers.' Your mom would tell mine, and I'd get it—when you were the one with the six candy bars!" Talk about lying! And I had forgotten all about it. I would have said that I have always been a very honest and straightforward person.

Consider these comments from Foodaholics in my workshops:

"I've stolen food. My kids have had food that was very clearly theirs, and I've chopped away at it until they asked where it went. Then I had to confess."

"I steal my roommates' food. Even if I have the same items, I go for theirs."

"I realized how serious my food problem was when I was caught stealing in my neighbors' kitchen. We don't lock doors. They live downstairs and are gone every day. I used to nibble their stuff until one day when they walked in and I had to find an excuse for my presence there."

"I'm a real estate broker, and we hold open house. I have taken home food from the refrigerator of a house we were showing."

Even if we never, or seldom, take other people's food, we may be reluctant to give our food to others. In fact, some of us Foodaholics cannot fathom how others can willingly relinquish a breast of chicken, a piece of pie, or the last of the chocolate sauce.

7. The Forced Feeder

4 3 2 1 0   Do you feel powerless over food?

4 3 2 1 0   Do you eat more than you planned? Examples: deciding on the antipasto, and then hearing yourself ask the waitress for lasagna; waking up resolved to go on a diet and realizing at 10 A.M. that you've just eaten a sweet roll.

4 3 2 1 0   Do you eat even when you're not hungry?

4 3 2 1 0   Do you eat foods you do not especially like? Example: finishing off a box of uninteresting or stale crackers or pretzels.

4 3 2 1 0   Do other people determine what you will eat? Examples: eating to please the host who keeps filling your plate; rewarding Grandma for making what she thinks is your favorite food by enthusiastically gobbling it and asking for more—even though you are actually not too fond of it.

Subtotal: _____

For a Foodaholic, not eating when food is around seems as hopeless as keeping dry when caught in a sudden shower. As one of my workshop participants told the others, "My brother adores whipped cream cake from a certain bakery. We always have it for his birthday. He looks forward to it immensely, and while he is eating, he smacks his lips and rants and raves about how marvelous it is. After a while, he puts his fork down, and while still extolling the virtues of this outstanding cake, he stops eating. I can't believe it! That he could quit while there's still some left seems unreal to me. It's something I didn't learn."

Of course, even normal eaters overeat at times. Example: Cecil succumbs to the seductiveness of a wide variety of foods by eating much more than usual, and his friends tease him about his "Smorgasbord smile." Under other circumstances, however, Cecil does not let food control him.

8. Feast or Famine

4 3 2 1 0   How frequently are you engaged in either an eating binge or an attempt to diet?

Subtotal: _____

Normal eaters who gain weight modify their intake for a while, bringing their weight back to its usual level. How frequently or how successfully do you diet? For many of us, battling for control over our eating is a consistent pattern.

9. Foodaholic Defenses

A. Denial: How Often Do You Tell Yourself?

4 3 2 1 0   Sure, I eat destructively. Doesn't everybody?

4 3 2 1 0   Sure, I live on junk food, but I'm not fat.

4 3 2 1 0   Lots of people eat more than I do.

4 3 2 1 0   My gorging didn't make me feel this awful. It's lack of sleep.

4 3 2 1 0   I skipped lunch (while eating 3000 calories to make up for it).

4 3 2 1 0   A little bit won't hurt (as you start on your favorite binge food).

4 3 2 1 0   I ate very little today (not counting snacks).

Subtotal: _____

These defenses are forms of *denial.* We deny the effects of our overeating. We deny our inability to control our binges, conning ourselves into believing that this time we can manage to eat moderate quantities of our addictive foods. We deny that all the little mouthfuls add up and that ten tiny slivers of cake equal one large slice.

B. Delusions

4 3 2 1 0   Other people tell me I'm much fatter/thinner than I think I am.

4 3 2 1 0   I used to be fat/thin, and I still picture myself that way.

4 3 2 1 0   I'm amazed at how fat/thin I look in photographs.

Subtotal: _____

These Foodaholic statements represent *delusions* about body image. The most profound example occurs among anorexics, who will tell you, in absolute sincerity, that they are fat and that they must lose more weight. They simply won't hear any contradictory opinions; they're obsessed with their perceived "fatness," even when they're very slender or downright emaciated.

C. Rigidity

4 3 2 1 0   I think my problems would be solved if I could just get organized, but other people insist I'm already over-organized.

4 3 2 1 0   I'm compulsively neat.

4 3 2 1 0   I have specific times for given activities, and I feel unnerved by deviations from my schedule.

4 3 2 1 0   I exercise rigorously and regularly, and when I can't, I feel very anxious.

4 3 2 1 0   Sitting still and relaxing is distressing for me.

4 3 2 1 0   If I do something wrong, I worry that everyone will think less of me.

4 3 2 1 0   There just aren't enough hours in the day for all I have to do.

Subtotal: _____

These are all examples of *rigidity*. Many Foodaholics make lots of lists. Our lives may be extremely structured. We have a fetish for neatness. We berate ourselves when we forget something or make a mistake. A change in our plans creates stress. We are so busy orchestrating our own lives and the lives of those around us that we leave little or no time for self-care, relaxation, and fun. So how do we take care of ourselves in the midst of all this self-induced pressure? By eating, of course. And what do we eat? Anything we can gobble on the run, usually processed junk foods. And when we eat "forbidden" foods, or don't maintain our diet perfectly, we tell ourselves we are hopeless failures who never do anything right. At that point we throw up our hands and go on a binge.

D. Blaming: Do You Tell Yourself or Others the Following?

4 3 2 1 0   We live in a food-oriented society; my eating is normal among my group.

4 3 2 1 0   Those tempting foods on TV are part of the problem.

4 3 2 1 0   The hostess will be hurt if I don't eat her food.

4 3 2 1 0   I have to have all that junk food around for my teen-agers.

4 3 2 1 0   My spouse is skinny and needs fattening foods.

4 3 2 1 0   My customers expect large, elaborate meals when I take them out.

Subtotal: _____

This defense system is called *blaming*. It aids us in proving to ourselves that circumstances and other people have more power than we do. "They" control us. We are putty in their hands.

E. Rationalization: How Often Do You Think?

4 3 2 1 0   Oh, well, it's a vacation.*

4 3 2 1 0   My family runs to fat, anyway.

4 3 2 1 0   I think it's my metabolism.

4 3 2 1 0   I haven't had pie for ages, so two pieces tonight is okay.*

4 3 2 1 0   After all, I've gotten rid of all my other vices. I have to have some fun in life.*

Subtotal: _____

Sound familiar? This defense mechanism is called *rationalization*. The starred items are also examples of "marshmallowing." This "sticky, patronizing, and seductive" voice sounds nurturing and supportive but is actually destructive.[2]

F. Self-Ridicule: Do You Say or Think?

4 3 2 1 0   I'm just a jolly, fat person.

4 3 2 1 0   Here comes the garbage disposal—me!

4 3 2 1 0   I'd be just the right weight if I were six inches taller.

4 3 2 1 0   You don't have to worry about leftovers when I'm around.

4 3 2 1 0   I'm not allowed to have second helpings. So I'll just skip them and go right to thirds.

Subtotal: _____

Self-Ridicule can also be a defense mechanism. Female Foodaholics are less likely to use this type of humor. For women, overeating and weight are usually taken very seriously. It could be these subjects are rarely discussed.

G. Intellectualizing: How Often Do You Tell Yourself or Others?

4 3 2 1 0   People in our family have a tendency to eat as a conflict avoidance mechanism.

4 3 2 1 0   Our culture is chemophilic, fondly believing that there is a substance to cure any problem.

4 3 2 1 0   The media and manufacturers establish the norms in our society by creating a demand for specific food products.

Subtotal: _____

Intellectualizing is a defense that enables us to avoid the emotions that accompany our condition and to distance ourselves from the problem. We talk about things, about others, and not about ourselves and how we contribute to our problem.

10. The Foodaholic's Best Friend

How often have these statements or similar ones been directed to you?

4 3 2 1 0   We're on vacation. I want to see the sights, not only the restaurants.

4 3 2 1 0   Don't eat now. There's a big meal coming.

4 3 2 1 0   A third helping? Where do you put it all?

4 3 2 1 0   How can you still be hungry? That meal was huge.

4 3 2 1 0   I was saving that piece of cake for Mitzi.

4 3 2 1 0   All we do is go out and eat. I want to do something different this weekend.

4 3 2 1 0   Your crunching all during the movie bothered me.

4 3 2 1 0   Yes, it's time for lunch, but we should complete our agenda before we break.

4 3 2 1 0   I know the food at LeGourmet is great, but we'll be late for the movie if we go there.

4 3 2 1 0   I'm so glad you picked up the prescription for Belinda's earache. Oh, I see you got a pizza, too. What—you forgot the prescription?

4 3 2 1 0   Yes, that dinner-theater serves good food, but they have rotten plays. What's more important, the food or the play?

4 3 2 1 0   It's true, this airline is notorious for its crummy cuisine. But I have never seen anyone get so thoroughly upset over a bad meal.

4 3 2 1 0   We keep talking about food, recipes, restaurants. Tell me, have you read any good books lately?

Subtotal: _____

If your food talk or behavior elicits such comments, or if, after repeated trips to the refrigerator or the buffet table, you turn around to find several pairs of eyes looking at you questioningly or accusingly, your relationship with food is having an unhealthy effect on your relationships with people.

Foodaholism Total: _____

SUGAR TOTAL

The Sugar Fix

4 3 2 1 0   Do you eat quantities of sweets and processed carbohydrates: cereals, bread, crackers, baked goods, chips, pretzels, candy, and soft drinks?

4 3 2 1 0   Do you lust after sweets? Are your hungers often specifically for sweets or processed carbohydrates?

4 3 2 1 0   Do you experience a rush of energy, a "high" or a similar stimulating response when you eat sweets?

4 3 2 1 0   Do you notice a mood change after eating sugar or foods containing sugar?

4 3 2 1 0   Does a sugar binge leave you enervated, depressed, or irritable several hours later or the next day?

4 3 2 1 0   Do you get sleepy within two to four hours after eating manufactured carbohydrates?

4 3 2 1 0   Do your cravings for and actual consumption of food increase after you eat foods that contain sugar?

4 3 2 1 0   Do you often eat sweets or processed carbohydrates instead of a nutritious meal?

4 3 2 1 0   Do you experience withdrawal symptoms—headache, shakiness, achiness, hot and cold spells, lethargy, insomnia—when you abstain from your sugary and starchy confections?

4 3 2 1 0   After going without all sugars and refined starches for at least a week, do you feel like a different person?

4 3 2 1 0   Do you eat sweets in secret?

4 3 2 1 0   Would you feel ashamed if others knew of your total sweets consumption?

4 3 2 1 0   Do you also shock yourself when you tally up several days' intake?

4 3 2 1 0   Do you arrange your life around getting a supply of sweets? For example: shopping at the grocery store that has the freshest, most appealing doughnuts; talking the office crew into lunching at the pie shop; shopping for candy bargains the day after Christmas, Easter, or Valentine's Day.

4 3 2 1 0   Do you cover your addiction by peddling your drug to others? Examples: keeping the candy dish on your desk filled for the boss and your co-workers; buying or baking sweets for co-workers, your family, or neighbors on every possible occasion and inventing a few new occasions; invariably including desserts, even at a wine and cheese party, a brunch, or a cocktail party.

Sugar Total: _____

Sugar addiction is a very real problem, one that can cause the sugar junkie to have difficulties with friends, co-workers, and family, as well as physical illnesses. Here's what some sugar junkies have observed about themselves:

"If I am monkeying with sugar at all, I have this problem with a co-worker, and I will yell at her across the room, 'Quit staring at me.' Normally I wouldn't do that."

"After I have gobbled down all the carbs in sight, I can't stand my husband. There is absolutely nothing he could say that would be all right with me. I dislike him so much at these times, I seriously consider divorce. The only thing that has kept us together is that I've recognized my irritability as sugar-induced. I keep promising myself that if I still want a divorce after I'm back on my 'clean' foods and have withdrawn from sugar, I will get it. But, of course, in the absence of my food-drugs, my husband emerges as a lovable man again. The same habits of his that drive me absolutely crazy when I'm 'using' seem pitifully inconsequential when I'm not."

TOTAL COST

1. Physical

4 3 2 1 0   Are you lethargic or chronically fatigued?

4 3 2 1 0   Is your food consumption aggravating your dental decay, blood pressure, diabetes, hypoglycemia, ulcer, heart condition, or other medical problem?

4 3 2 1 0   Is there a correlation between your headaches and food abuse?

4 3 2 1 0   Do you eat the kinds or quantities of food that make you sleepy?

4 3 2 1 0   Could your eating patterns be causing insomnia?

4 3 2 1 0   Do you have physical symptoms that are alleviated when you eat only moderate quantities and only nourishing foods?

4 3 2 1 0   Is your endurance diminished by what you eat?

Subtotal: _____

Some recovering Foodaholics report remission or improvement of their arthritis or migraines so long as they eliminate junk foods. They frequently experience flare-ups after a binge.

2. Emotional

4 3 2 1 0   Do you feel ashamed and guilty?

4 3 2 1 0   Do certain foods leave you depressed?

4 3 2 1 0   Anxious?

4 3 2 1 0   Agitated or hyperactive?

4 3 2 1 0   Irritable?

4 3 2 1 0   Does eating certain foods cause you to behave in ways that you consider strange or insane?

Subtotal: _____

Lorraine: I feel trapped like a rat in a maze. I just want to run and run.

Salina: I wake up in the middle of the night terror-stricken. I feel a real gasping kind of panic about little things that normally would barely cause me a twinge.

Wendell: My roommate gets suicidal after a big binge. After I mentioned it to a friend of mine, he described someone he knows who is like that, too.

3. Intellectual

4 3 2 1 0   Do you feel confused or lacking in mental clarity? The experience may feel similar to having a word on the tip of your tongue, and not being able to connect with it. The difference is, now it's your mind that won't make the connection. I used to be puzzled when playing bridge after I demolished the bowlful of candy; the game felt more foreign than familiar.

4 3 2 1 0   Do you have poor concentration or reduced attention span?

4 3 2 1 0   Does nibbling or being obsessed with food prevent you from focusing on your reading, studies, or projects?

Subtotal: _____

Pat: I sit in class mentally looking over the choices in the vending machines and planning my snack. If we don't break at the usual time, I'm no longer listening.

Lettie: I notice I make more mistakes in my work. It's like working through a fog. I can do most of it, but I struggle to stay focused.

Mary: I know I am an intelligent woman. I wanted to finish my education, but believed my poor concentration would be an obstacle. I blamed it on the aging process and was ready to relinquish my dream. A couple of months after I designed and followed a healthy eating program, my brain began to behave "youthfully" again!

Total Cost: _____

SCORING INDEX

The three different scores you have obtained each have a significance. Your Foodaholism Total is an indication of the degree of your obsession with food and defensiveness about that problem. The Sugar Total measures your addiction to sweets or processed carbohydrates such as bread, crackers, baked goods, chips, pretzels, candy, soft drinks, and highly processed cereals. Your Total Cost is a barometer of the price you pay physically, emotionally, and mentally for your food abuse.

Scores that fall below these levels are normal:

Foodaholism Total	115
Sugar Total	22
Total Cost	22

Foodaholism Total

Below 115: You aren't a Foodaholic, although you may have occasional bouts of less-than-healthy eating. Your real problem may be how unforgiving you are of yourself for that behavior.

115-130: You have a tendency toward Foodaholism. Review your test scores and note if there is one *specific* area in which you score relatively high, or have a cluster of 3's or 4's. If this is your scoring pattern, you could be a single-issue Foodaholic, and specific sections of this book may be particularly important to you. It is also possible that you are less than 15 percent overweight, and keep inflicting a diet on yourself and then rebelling. You might stop abusing food if you stopped scolding yourself and simply allowed yourself to eat healthy foods and quantities. Perhaps you are a person who was reared with constant comments about what you did or did not eat, and now you are continuing the same running commentary in your head. Were you to send this Resident Critic in your head on a Hawaiian vacation, your preoccupation with food might diminsh noticeably. Read Chapters 10 through 14 of this book—then read them again!

130-170: You are a full-scale Foodaholic. Please read the book thoughtfully and work your program well. Remember, you probably did not develop your destructive eating patterns overnight. Do not be impatient or unfair to yourself by expecting an immediate recovery and lifestyle change.

Sugar Total and Total Cost

If either or both of these figures are above 22, a carbohydrate intolerance or an allergic reaction to specific foods may be contributing to your food cravings and destructive eating. The three-step program outlined in Chapter 2 may help you identify foods that are creating problems for you. As an experiment, treat such foods as poison for a time—avoid them completely—then note whether your Foodaholism subsides and you subsequently begin to eat normally. Be sure to read Chapters 3, 4, and 5.

A Total Cost that falls within the normal range (22 or below), combined with high totals for Foodaholism or Sugar, is a suspicious score. Unquestionably, there *are* consequences to which you are unattuned. Being accustomed to feeling marginal or being inattentive to the negative effects doesn't lessen these effects or consequences of unhealthy eating.

Another possibility is that you find certain patterns of thinking or behaving unacceptable, and won't permit yourself to acknowledge them. You may have a strong system of denial. Recheck your denial answers in the questionnaire.

For a clearer picture of your Destructive Eating Index, chart your scores using Figure 1-1. Place your Foodaholism Total opposite the appropriate number on the first line, your Sugar Total on the middle line, and your Total Cost on the third line. Now draw lines connecting your Fooda-

FIGURE 1-1 Destructive Eating Index.

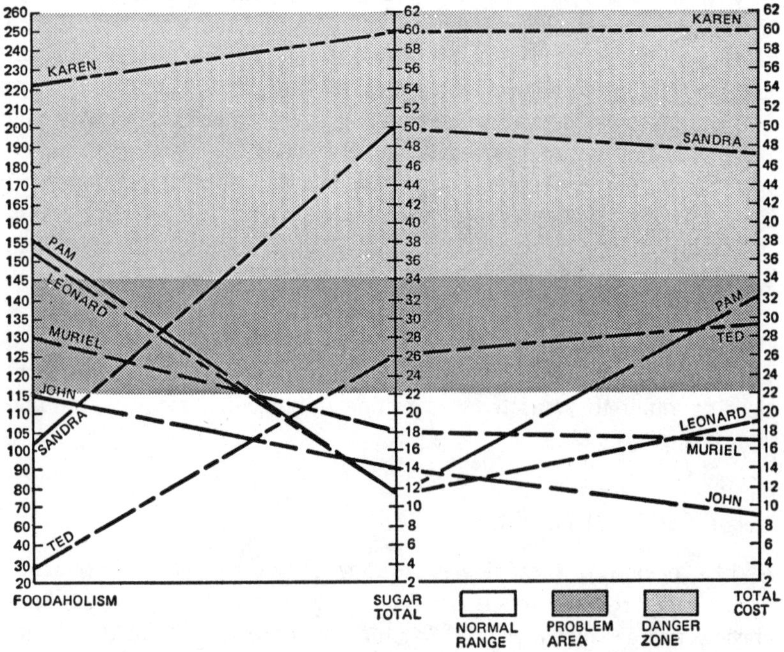

NAME	FOODAHOLISM	SUGAR TOTAL	TOTAL COST
KAREN	222	60	60
PAM	156	11	32
LEONARD	154	11	19
MURIEL	130	18	17
JOHN	115	14	9
SANDRA	102	50	47
TED	27	26	29
SCALES	20-260	2-62	2-62
INCREMENTS	VARIABLE	2	2

holism, Sugar Total, and Total Cost scores. Notice how your scores relate to the following profiles:

Ted (27-26-29): Ted is not a Foodaholic, but he is diagnosed hypoglycemic. When his blood sugar level is low, he becomes disoriented, confused, and fairly incapacitated. He has blacked out a few times. Ted needs to eat preventively to keep his blood sugar at a normal level, but unlike a Foodaholic, he has difficulty remembering to do that. He has to remind himself with notes.

John (115-14-9): John is a single-issue Foodaholic. His score in the rigidity area was 26. John's rigidity resulted in his Food Fixation score being higher, too, because when John deviates slightly from his rigid menu, he is merciless with himself. His critical internal dialogue causes him to think more about food.

Sandra (102-50-47): This is my own profile. I have been working my program as a recovering Foodaholic for seven years and am celebrating my ex-perfectionism, reduced preoccupation with food, and my less food-oriented lifestyle. When I deviate from my Healthy Eating Program by eating sweets or starchy junk foods, I pay a very high price. These substances are stressors for me. With my heightened level of body awareness I can clearly define unhealthy foods and quantities.

Muriel (130-18-17): Muriel is a tall, muscular woman who works hard, plays hard, eats enthusiastically and nutritiously, and regularly lifts weights to keep in shape. She weighs nearly 200 pounds and is forever talking about dieting. Muriel is substantially built, rather than obese. She is so thoroughly disgusted with her weight that she disregards how well she looks and feels, and the fact that muscle weighs more than fat. She would not be obsessed with food if she stopped trying to change her body type.

Pam (156-12-32): Pam is a Foodaholic but not a sugar junkie. She neither craves sugar, nor reacts negatively to it. She does pay a price for eating too much or for eating foods containing sulfur. Pam buys unsulfured, organically-grown produce. She has designed an eating program consisting of unprocessed, unadulterated foods which please her.

Leonard (154-11-19): With such a high Destructive Eating Total, Leonard is building a lot of his life around food. His low Total Cost indicates that he is cutting himself off from or mistrusting the sensations of his body as well as his emotional ups and downs. This denial of self in order to focus on external factors such as one's achievements or others' needs is a typical pattern of martyrdom or machodom.

Karen (222-60-60): Karen is a blatant and obvious sugar junkie. Other people can describe for her how she behaves differently with or without sweet stuff in her life. She even looks different! She herself notices the changes in her energy and irritability depending on what she eats. Although she feels happier and more peaceful without empty carbohydrates in her life, she rarely maintains such an eating plan for long because she seriously questions her *right* to feel that happy and peaceful. Being self-destructive and allowing others to use her for a doormat are also part of the pattern. Karen's recovery depends on her working through those therapy issues and developing a Healthy Eating and Lifestyle Program.

NOTES

1. Original adaptation of a 10-item assessment of drinking problems to an inventory of food problems was by Victoria Holbert, Minneapolis Community College, Minneapolis, MN.
2. Jean Illsley Clarke, *Self-Esteem: A Family Affair.* (Minneapolis, MN: Winston Press, 1978), pp. 268–269.

2
The Foodaholic
Blame Plan
or Setup for Sabotage

If you've completed and scored the Foodaholism Questionnaire, you probably have more insights into your destructive eating patterns than I did seven years ago. Here's how I remember realizing that I was a Foodaholic:

THE BIG CON

I used to tell myself: "If I didn't have to watch my husband eating all the time, I'd be okay. If I didn't have to cook and sit down to those huge meals, I'd eat less." I promised myself during his business trips the children and I would eat simple, healthy foods in moderate quantities.

So then he'd travel, and we would eat tuna, omelets, and fruit with cheese—right? Wrong! It was more like spaghetti, tacos, and pizza. "Well," I thought, "it's the old problem of having to have foods kids like. I wouldn't be eating all that stuff if I didn't have to please them."

Inevitably the week arrived when everyone was away. Now was my chance to eat small, low-calorie meals. I did do that, but also foraged between meals. I gained weight that week. Now I was speechless, fresh out of excuses.

That's when I finally admitted that I was an authentic Foodaholic. Later I realized that I also ate destructively when I was both happy and unhappy. And I have plenty of company. We Foodaholics commonly associate food with fun, food with parties, food with vacations, and food with all of life's celebrations.

Our eating pattern includes staying close to the buffet table at cocktail parties and nibbling incessantly. My preference is rich, gooey hors d'oeuvres and desserts. We chomp our way through a movie, a television program, or a good book. We actually plan to return from a vacation dragging our added pounds and overstuffed bodies.

We Foodaholics may think weekends are a time for visiting special places and eating special foods. Even when we don't go anywhere special, we manage to keep ourselves supplied with our special foods. "After all," we figure, "what other amusement is available when I'm having such a dull weekend?" Ironically then, the weekend becomes even *more* boring or depressing because we feel progressively worse physically and mentally as a natural consequence of our destructive eating.

Sometimes I nibbled so incessantly as a part of my normal weekend eating behavior that I would arrive at a gala dinner party already full. That usually didn't stop me from enthusiastically participating in demolishing the high-calorie creations. After all, I wouldn't want to hurt my host's feelings, would I? And I had been looking forward to this gourmet dinner for weeks, salivating over my vivid recollections of my host's exotic creations. Of course, it wasn't nearly as much fun as I had fantasized, because I wasn't hungry enough to enjoy it.

I kept telling myself that I ate for pleasure. Food was one of my main joys in life. It's my only vice. And after all, I have to eat to live. But isn't it strange? Here I am eating all this food, all these calories, gaining all these pounds with very little pleasure. No wonder I needed more and more food. The enjoyment I was seeking wasn't really there.

When I share this pattern, which I call my *"set-up for sabotage,"* with members of the Foodaholic groups or classes, they start nodding their heads. One by one, they begin listing all the conditions under which they eat destructively. As our collective list grows, we become acutely aware of our personal reasons for destructive eating, as well as reasons we share with other members of the group. Gradually, we see ourselves more clearly through others and we come face to face with the hard, cold reality of our Foodaholism.

We have a problem—an eating problem. We are compulsive eaters who have been hiding behind a multitude of excuses. We have been conning ourselves and maybe everyone else, too. We have been copping out! We have been using all these reasons and excuses to avoid acknowledging the magnitude of our problem, to avoid our own responsibility for it, and to avoid doing anything about it.

CONDITIONS
FOR DESTRUCTIVE EATING

How about your excuses? I invite you quickly and impulsively to list below all the conditions under which you eat destructively. In doing this, you might find out something important about yourself.

_____   _____

_____   _____

_____   _____

_____   _____

_____   _____

Now go through the following list and put a check mark next to the answers that match yours. Go back over this list and check any additional items that apply to you:

angry	can't wake up
anxious	feeling inadequate
bored	in transition or limbo
frustrated	lonely
tense	sexy
tired	celebrating
can't sleep	vacationing
stressed	pleasing others
Clean Plate Club	depressed
it's there	scared
it's time	resentful
might _get_ hungry	rebellious
for energy	revengeful
to calm down	empty
procrastinating	unloved
avoiding	rejected

How about hunger? Was feeling hungry on your original list? Is it one of the least frequent or important reasons for eating? Or do you eat preventively in order to avoid actually feeling your hunger? Is hunger just another of the many feelings you choose to sedate rather than to feel? Are you using food to seek a state of partial or complete numbness?

Count your check marks. How many of the conditions listed apply to you? Six? Ten? Twelve? More than twelve? What do you make of this score? What do you think it means?

FINDING EXCUSES

At first, when I ask folks to notice the conditions under which they over-eat, they describe binging when:

- Mom is doing her "hovering mother" routine.
- My spouse or boss is being critical.
- There's nothing better to do.
- My plans have fallen through.

At such times we think: Poor me, what else can I do under such awful circumstances? Then I eat to:

- Soothe myself.
- Amuse myself.
- Abuse myself.
- Fill my deep-down emptiness.

I eat because I'm adjusting to a (an):

- Move.
- New job.
- Empty nest.
- Promotion.
- Difficult project.
- Deadline.

I eat because I have to learn to live with a new:

- Roommate.
- Spouse.
- Stepchild.

I eat when I'm stressed by:

- My divorce.
- A sick parent.
- A demanding child.
- A tough boss.
- A petty co-worker.
- Interfering relatives.
- An unresponsive mate.
- The end of a love affair.
- Raising teenagers.

THE BLAME GAME

Jane Noland, author of *Laugh It Off,* humorously lists some more situations to blame:

"My parents for my body type."

"The local fast-food place for establishing itself within walking distance of home."

"The world economy for driving up the prices of high-protein foods and fresh produce. Here I can be more specific, blaming heads of state, legislators (especially those of the opposite political party), drought, locusts, strikes, or the IRS."

"My favorite uncle, who introduced me, at the greedy and impressionable age of two and a half to the addictive pleasures of the soda fountain, thus launching me on a lifelong course of equating food with good times."

"The phone company for installing a stretch cord that extends to the refrigerator."

"The Girl Scouts for selling cookies."

"The Persians for discovering how to process sugar cane juice into solid sugar."

"My kids, who douse me with guilt when I am not being a 'good-mother-who-bakes.' "

"My mother for *being* a 'good-mother-who-bakes.' "

"My 'good-grandmother-who bakes' who taught my 'good-mother-who-bakes' who taught *me* . . . etc., etc., ad rotundum."[1]

THE BIG CON REVISITED

Life seems to be chock full of stresses and temptations, doesn't it? There's always an excuse handy when we want to blame our destructive eating on a source outside ourselves. The hard, cold truth is we use food to handle much of life, as a coping mechanism for many situations, both positive and negative. We use all our excuses to kid ourselves that circumstances or other people have the power to legislate what we eat.

We may be avoiding responsibility for our behavior because:

- It can help us, in at least a partial sense, to not quite grow up.
- It can nourish our need to feel victimized, martyred, or self-sacrificing.
- It may be the only way in which we allow ourselves to exercise spontaneity or impulsiveness.
- It could be helping us to avoid the uncomfortable feelings that often accompany separation and differentiation from others. We may confuse this natural growth process with disloyalty.
- It may prove how helpless or hopeless we are.

Whatever your personal payoff for escaping responsibility for your eating behavior, you *do have* the power to change. I strongly urge you to refrain from scolding yourself:

> "You turkey, you're at it again."
> "You are thoroughly irresponsible."
> "You slob, you ate the whole thing just 'cause it was left over."

Rarely does such negative feedback motivate positive change. More likely, you will only succeed in diminishing your self-esteem.

EXPERIMENT IN AWARENESS

The following three-step, three-week program may help you change your thinking and heighten your body awareness in a positive way. I recommend that you start your program with these procedures:

Week 1

Use the worksheet (Table 2-1) to keep a journal of everything you eat. Don't change your usual patterns, and don't berate yourself if the amount

TABLE 2-1
FOOD JOURNAL

HOW I FEEL BEFORE I EAT		RATE HUNGER (1–10)	WHAT I EAT (INCLUDE QUANTITY)	WHERE I EAT (STANDING, SITTING)	HOW I FEEL AFTERWARD	
Physically	Emotionally				Physically	Emotionally

of food you list is surprisingly large. At the same time, review the Total Cost questions in the Foodaholism Questionnaire, so you can keep in mind what you are looking for. Then summarize in the first two columns of the Food Journal how you feel—physically and emotionally—prior to eating a certain food; use the last two columns to record your emotional and physical data after eating. Your answers may give you some clues as to which foods are genuinely bad for you, unrelated to calorie counts. Observe what situations or emotions you attempt to medicate or soothe with food, and keep track of how well this strategy works for you. Do you achieve the mood changes you seek? For how long? How do you feel the next hour or day after a specific food is eaten? Notice how hungry you feel prior to eating. Rate yourself on a hunger scale from 0-10, and place your rating in the third column.

Week 2

Eat whatever you normally do. In addition, before you eat tell yourself:
"I am eating this simply because I want to" or "Right now I choose to eat this."

This exercise will sharpen your awareness of how you feel when you take responsibility for your decisions and choices instead of defensively supplying yourself with reasons or excuses for destructive eating.

Week 3

During this week, you may eat *only* when it is pleasurable for you. Take the time to really *be* with your food. Look at it, smell it, handle it if you like. Take a little while to appreciate it before you eat it, and then taste it thoroughly and well; notice its flavors, texture, consistency. Feel yourself chewing it, swallowing it. Feel it going down and imagine it in your stomach.

During this week you are to notice what flavors, textures, and consistencies are most satisfying or pleasurable for you. I discovered during this exercise that I especially like chewy and crunchy foods. I can overdose on sundaes and pies, but I don't feel satisfied until my mouth and teeth work hard on my food.

In order to focus on your food, delay reading and watching television until after eating. Some of you may need to eat alone if you find the presence of others very distracting. When certain folks are around, you may not taste what you eat.

Have fun during this third week! Return to the Foodaholism Questionnaire and notice how much you have improved already—physically, mentally, and emotionally. While you are enjoying yourself, this may be a good time to read the information contained in the sections on "Foodaholism and Physical Addiction" and "The Foodaholic Way of Life." "Getting Well: Changing Lifestyles" offers specific exercises and assignments to help you change your Foodaholic attitudes and behavior. How successfully you change will probably correlate with how thoughtfully and conscientiously you *help* yourself—how carefully you build your own *Healthy Eating* and *Lifestyle Program*.

Working your program along with a friend or a small group of supportive people can multiply your dividends. Healthy people would not support your playing psychological games and would confront you if you said:

- Oh that's silly, I'll just skip part of my program.
- There's nothing I can do about that.
- It's hopeless.
- I'm helpless.

There are always at least several options, even in the most demanding situation. Friends may see those more clearly than you do. Be aware, though, that if you say or think "yes-but" or "no-but" in response to several suggestions, you really want to stay stuck. It's better to brainstorm options without judging or evaluating; write them down and then pick the best one a day or two later.

Changing is sometimes scary for us and threatening to those around us. A strong support system can ease our path. The most important criterion for a healthy support system is that it encourages and nourishes our growth, not our powerlessness or passivity. It is important that you select the type of people most apt to truly support you as you change. The information in Chapter 10, especially the sections "Discharging Your Jury and Helpers" and "Turning Food Buddies into Friends" can help you avoid destructive choices for membership in your healthy support system.

NOTES

1. Jane Thomas Noland, *Laugh It Off, A Self-discovery Workbook for Weight Losers.* (Minneapolis, MN: © CompCare Publications, 1979), pp. 9–10. Used by permission of the author and CompCare Publications, Minneapolis, MN.

II

FOODAHOLISM AND PHYSICAL ADDICTION

3
Sugar
as a Drug

Sugar is, by definition, a drug: a "substance other than food intended to affect the structure or function of the body."[1] When abused, sugar can become a lethal drug, just like alcohol, tranquilizers, barbiturates, and amphetamines. As potentially addictive as heroin, and just as deadly when consumed in quantity over a long period, this toxic agent has caused untold disease and suffering. According to Dr. John Yudkin: "If only a small fraction of what is already known about the effects of sugar were to be revealed in relation to any other material used as a food additive, that material would promptly be banned."[2]

Our ancestors survived on animal and plant life. They did not have to contend with the packaged, processed, chemically flavored and preserved excuses for food that we consume today. They used sugar sparingly; rather than a staple, it was a luxury.

Until this century, sugar was not considered a food. It was used as a seasoning, like salt or pepper. Only after the development of fast and inexpensive refinement methods did sugar become what Dr. David Reuben calls "the most commonly used adulterating chemical in the processing of food." Sugar is heavy and provides food manufacturers with a cheap filler.

The main ingredient in many cake and pastry mixes is not flour but sugar. Many brands of ice cream use more sugar than cream.[3] Table 3-1, Hidden Sugar, and Table 3-2, Sugar Content of Cereals, show the high percentage of sugar in other foods.

Our bodies are simply not equipped to handle the onslaught of sugar —in all its forms—that is part of our current lifestyle. Food processing has

TABLE 3-1
HIDDEN SUGAR[4]

PERCENTAGE OF SUGAR IN COMMON FOODS:

Foods	Percentages
Del Monte Whole Kernel Corn	10.7
Libby's Peaches	17.9
Quaker 100% Natural Cereal	24
Skippy Peanut Butter	9.2
Sealtest Chocolate Ice Cream	21
Cool Whip	21
Dannon Blueberry Yogurt	17.7
Coffee-Mate	65
Cremora	56.9
Heinz Tomato Ketchup	29
Ragú Spaghetti Sauce	6.2
Wish-Bone Russian Dressing	30
Wish-Bone Italian Dressing	7.3
Wish-Bone French Dressing	23
Wyler's Bouillon Cubes	14.8
Hamburger Helper	23
Shake 'n Bake Barbecue Style	51
Shake 'n Bake Original	17.4
Shake 'n Bake Italian	14.7
Ritz Crackers	12
Coca-Cola	8.8
Cherry Jell-o	82.6
Hershey's Chocolate Bar	51
Sara Lee Chocolate Cake	35.9

TABLE 3-2
SUGAR CONTENT OF DRY CEREALS[5]

	% SUCROSE AND OTHER SUGARS
Quaker Oats Shredded Wheat	0
Nabisco Spoon-sized Shredded Wheat	0
Uncle Sam Cereal	0
Nabisco Shredded Wheat	0
Puffed Rice	0
Puffed Wheat	0
Cheerios	4
Toasted Mini Wheats	4
Special K	7
Kix	7
Kellogg Corn Flakes	7
Wheat Chex	7
Rice Chex	7
Corn Chex	7
Post Toasties	7
Ralston Purina Corn Flakes	7
Concentrate	10
Total	10
Corn Total	10
Product 19	10
General Mills Country Corn Flakes	10
Wheaties	10
Grape Nuts	10
Skinner Raisin Bran	10
Crispy Rice	10
Rice Krispies	10
Grape Nuts Flakes	14
Pep Wheat Flakes	14
Life	18
Buc Wheats	18

GOOD (LOW SUGAR) — (bracket grouping rows Quaker Oats Shredded Wheat through Rice Krispies)

FAIR — (bracket grouping rows Grape Nuts Flakes through Buc Wheats)

TABLE 3-2 (continued)

		% SUCROSE AND OTHER SUGARS
	Bran Chex	18
	Post 40% Bran Flakes	18
	Team	18
	Sun Country Granola	20
	Fortified Oat Flakes	21
	100% Bran	21
	Nature Valley Granola/Coconut & Honey	21
	Nature Valley Granola/Oats & Honey	21
	All Bran	21
	Country Morning/Raisins & Dates	21
FAIR (MODERATE SUGAR)	100% Natural Cereal	21
	Kellogg 40% Bran Flakes	25
	Nature Valley Granola/Cinnamon / Raisins	25
	Country Morning	25
	Most	28
	Frosted Mini Wheats	28
	100% Natural Cereal/Apples & Cinnamon	28
	Nature Valley Granola/Fruit & Nuts	28
	Cracklin Bran	28
	100% Natural Cereal/Raisins & Dates	32
	Post Raisin Bran	32
	Bran Buds	32
	Ralston Purina Raisin Bran	32
	Honey Nut Cheerios	35
	Trix	35
	Captain Crunch Peanut Butter Cereal	35
	Heartland	—
	Heartland/Raisins	—
POOR	Graham Crackos	39
	Lucky Charms	39
	Alpha-Bits	39
	Frosted Rice	39

TABLE 3-2 (continued)

		% SUCROSE AND OTHER SUGARS
	Kellogg Sugar Frosted Corn Flakes	39
	Ralston Purina Sugar Frosted Flakes	39
	Golden Grahams	39
	Frosty O's	39
	Cocoa Puffs	39
	Honeycomb	39
	King Vitaman	42
	Kaboom	42
	Strawberry Crazy Cow	42
	Chocolate Crazy Cow	42
POOR (HIGH SUGAR)	Fruit Brute	42
	Captain Crunch	42
	Quisp	42
	Cookie Crisp	42
	Chocolate Cookie Crisp	46
	Vanilla Cookie Crisp	46
	Kellogg Raisin Bran	46
	Count Chocula	46
	Sugar (corn) Pops	46
	Frankenberry	46
	Captain Crunch Crunchberries	46
	Boo Berry	46
	Corny Snaps	46
	Cocoa Krispies	46
	Fruity Pebbles	46
	Cocoa Pebbles	46
	Frosted Rice Krinkles	46
	Super Sugar Crisp	49
	Fruit Loops	49
	Sugar Smacks	56
	Apple Jacks	56

accelerated beyond our bodies' tolerances, causing physical reactions which add to the social and emotional aspects of Foodaholism. For some of us, recovery from Foodaholism is not likely until we recognize and deal with the harmful effects certain substances have on our body chemistry. Sugar is the most commonly used of these potentially harmful substances.

Sugar is *not* food. It does *not* nourish us. It contains none of the vitamins, minerals, amino acids, or essential fatty acids that our bodies need for maintenance, repair, and growth.

Being a substance other than food and one that is also "intended to affect the function of the body," sugar aptly fits the definition of "drug." "Sugar junkies" use a "fix" of sweets to produce a surge of energy, a "high." Manufacturers and advertisers trade on that idea. They want us to believe that sugar produces energy. (It does, to the extent that the body needs calories to fuel it.) What manufacturers and advertisers *don't* tell us is that for many people, sugar provides an artificial, temporary, chemically-induced lift, followed by a depression of energy and emotions. Sugar may build some of us up, only to let us down.

ADDICTION

To understand why sugar is so addictive, we must take a look at how our bodies use it.

What we commonly call sugar is actually refined sugar—sucrose or fructose. But another form of sugar, "glucose" or "blood sugar," is the basic source of energy in our bodies. Glucose is fuel for our bodies as gasoline is fuel for our cars. A car won't run when it's out of gas; it won't run if the engine is flooded either. In the same way, our bodies (and our brains) function efficiently only if we have just the right level of glucose in our bloodstream, generally about 80 to 100 milligrams per 100 milliliters of blood.

The hormone insulin makes it possible for glucose (blood sugar) to enter nearly all the cells of the body, where it is used as an energy source. Unfortunately, the body does not always function ideally or as a finely adjusted mechanism. Dr. Richard Kunin, president of the Orthomolecular Medical Society, describes sugar metabolism in his book *Meganutrition:*[6]

> When you eat sugar and your blood sugar level goes up, your pan-creas secretes insulin to counteract the rise. The pancreas is the

blood sugar level monitor, so to speak, and restores the balance. But this is the problem: the pancreas is a monumental overachiever, especially when it meets a refined sugar that is readily absorbed into the bloodstream. Insulin that the pancreas shoots into your bloodstream to counteract the sugar overdose works so quickly and efficiently that it creates a *drop* in blood sugar levels before a balance can be restored.

It is this drop in blood sugar levels (see Figure A–3, Appendix A) that gives sugar its addictive effect: the body signals the drop with hunger, or "craving" for another "fix." The sugar junkie satisfies the craving with more sugar, and the cycle begins all over again. This downward spiral of energy and emotions is also a common pattern in chemical dependency. Sugar abuse parallels chemical dependence in other ways. In his book about addictive behavior, *How Much Is too Much?*, Stanton Peele outlines five "characteristics of an addictive experience." Notice whether your abusive eating patterns compare with these characteristics:

> *It eradicates awareness.* To create the addiction cycle, a drug experience must eliminate a person's sense of pain by lessening his awareness of what is hurting or troubling him.
>
> *It hurts other involvements.* The addiction cycle worsens when a drug experience makes a person less concerned about or less able to deal with other responsibilities. The person then turns increasingly toward the drug experience as his one source of gratification.
>
> *It lowers self-esteem.* The chief casualty of an addictive experience is the addict's regard for himself.
>
> *It is not pleasurable.* A popular misconception about drug addiction is that an addict takes a drug for pleasure. There is nothing pleasurable about the addiction cycle ... In fact, then, what is "pleasurable" about addiction is the *absence* of feelings and thoughts that lead to pain. The experience is not one of *positive* pleasurable sensation.
>
> *It is predictable.* Powerful depressant drugs are so effective as addictive objects not only because they lessen pain, but because they invariably produce the *same* effect.[7]

HYPOGLYCEMIA AND DIABETES

Eventually, repeated overdoses of sugar can lead to two kinds of chronic malfunction in the body: hypoglycemia and diabetes. In *hypoglycemia,* which is explained in greater detail in the next chapter, the body continues to overproduce insulin. Progressively, the body overreacts to a wider range of processed foods, creating a blood sugar level generally too low for proper functioning. In *diabetes,* the overworked pancreas ceases to produce enough insulin, and blood sugar levels become too high for proper functioning. Dr. Kunin estimates: "About one person in every six will eventually develop outright diabetes by adopting the present diet of Western civilization which is so high in sucrose and in refined carbohydrates. The number of people who are pre-diabetic and pre-hypoglycemic is more likely to be three out of five.[8]

Many authorities do not recommend the Glucose Tolerance Test (GTT), used to diagnose hypoglycemia and diabetes, for people over 70 because sugar intolerance is so common by that age. Dr. Kunin writes: "This is one of those circular diagnoses by which anything common is considered normal and hence tolerable—like tooth decay"[9] (which is also worsened by eating and drinking sugary substances).

Diabetes and hypoglycemia aren't the only problems that have been linked to excess sugar intake. Here are just a few others:

MALNUTRITION

As I have already said, sugar contains none of the vital nutrients that our bodies need for maintenance, growth, and repair. And when we meet our calorie needs with sugar, we are less likely to eat nutritious foods like meat, fish, vegetables, fruits, whole grains, dairy products, nuts, and seeds.

The body requires nutrients such as vitamin B to metabolize sugar. Taken alone and in large doses, sugar can rob our bodies of vitamin B and other vital nutrients. Furthermore, chronic sugar abuse alters our metabolism and our body chemistry so that we are less able to use nutrients.[10]

OBESITY

A lot of calories are packed into small amounts of sweet food. This caloric density is no substitute for the amount of food or bulk needed to satiate hunger. Consequently, caloric requirements are again likely to be exceeded and the excess stored as body fat. The insulin used to neutralize blood sugar also transports fat into body cells, promoting obesity.

HEART DISEASE

Sugar not only produces excess body fat, but also, when eaten in large amounts, increases the fatty material in the blood (triglycerides). Biochemist Richard Passwater concludes that triglycerides are a more important contributing factor in heart disease than is cholesterol. "A person eating a scant four ounces of sugar daily, from *all* sources, including natural ones, has more than five times the chance of having heart disease than someone eating only half as much sugar."[11] And yet FDA figures suggest the average is nearly six ounces,[12] equal to over one-third of a pound and 600 calories.

"Sugar may also contribute to heart disease by increasing the blood pressure-raising effects of a high-salt diet," writes *The New York Times* health columnist, Jane Brody.[13]

ALCOHOLISM

Biochemist Dr. Roger Williams carried out experiments which proved that the wrong diet can create an alcoholic.[14] Animals fed high-sugar diets showed a marked addiction to alcohol. In contrast, many recovering alcoholics report reduced cravings for alcohol after they eliminate sugar and eat healthy foods.

It is ironic and unfortunate that some chemical dependency counselors and individual members of Alcoholics Anonymous are among the most active promoters of sugar. Recovering alcoholics are shown how to substitute sweets when they crave a drink. Yet, when their blood sugar level drops, they experience the dry drunk syndrome: increased cravings, depression, fatigue, and irritability.

Without nutritional treatment of their disease, recovering alcoholics continue to "fall off the wagon" in great numbers, to require repeated treatment efforts, and to experience a far more painful and uncomfortable sobriety than is necessary.

EMOTIONAL PROBLEMS

The twice-divorced author of *Marital Choices*,[15] William Lederer, cites his own and his clients' faulty body chemistry as one of the factors in mar-

TOXIC WASTE
SITE

riage problems and divorce. He notes the increased negativity and irritability which can result from the hypoglycemic effect of falling blood sugar level.

Sugar intolerance seems to be a factor in a variety of neuroses as well as in children's behavioral and learning problems. The New York Institute for Child Development found 74 percent of children tested showed these latter effects.[16] Informal research at the Foodaholics' Treatment Center in Minneapolis links sugar abuse with food obsession. We are eager to have this correlation tested by rigorous research methods.

We Foodaholics struggle to cope with stress in our lives. We may even attend stress management seminars to enhance our coping skills. Then we eat to ease our feelings of stress, usually sweets and manufactured carbohydrates. Ironically, these foods are stressors, the most commonly occurring ones in our environment. What havoc we wreak upon ourselves!

BELINDA'S STORY

A former participant in the Foodaholics' Treatment Program, Belinda is a recovering sugar junkie who shared her conclusions about how sugar affected her. Prior to her vacation, she had abstained from sugar and white flour for five months. She continued during her holidays although she did

not attempt to diet. A day or two before Belinda's vacation ended, she told herself it would be a pity to miss her once-in-a-lifetime chance to try the unusual Spanish desserts. "Besides," she conned herself, "I can handle them now. I'm not a sugar junkie anymore."

"I fell off the wagon with a resounding thud for two whole months," Belinda recalls. "I returned home totally exhausted, even though the vacation had been a restful one. I told myself it was jet lag. I kept assuring myself I was handling the problem well. I would only eat sugar a little bit or once in a while."

"It took some time before it dawned on me. The 'little bits' were equaling a lot of sugar. A few bites of cake several times over equals a piece of cake. Eating sweets every day is not 'once in a while.' I wasn't feeling so well anymore. And my tiredness didn't always correlate with lack of sleep or working too hard. I finally had to admit that I was still a sugar junkie, and that I was hooked again."

Even with that realization, it took Belinda some time to get the "monkey" off her back. She finally succeeded after she experienced a flare-up of an old adversary—arthritis. She couldn't prove the arthritis was caused by sweets and other junk foods. "But," recalls Belinda, "I hurt enough to be willing to eliminate my favorite drugs if that change could make me feel better. I climbed back on the wagon, and my arthritis went back into remission. I know every time I slip a little and start toying with sweets, I will soon wake up in the morning with a sore finger or toe that tells me, 'You've been lying to yourself again. I won't let you get away with that.' "

TESTING YOUR ADDICTION

If you suspect you are a sugar or junk food junkie, or if you want to prove that you aren't, experiment with eliminating sugar from your diet for a week. That means cutting out sugar in all its guises. Refer to Table 4-3, page 67 for a guide to varieties of sugar. Eliminate processed chips and crackers as well as baked goods and candy.

Perhaps after a day or so without sugar or refined carbohydrates your hunger for sweets—your cravings—will seem to dominate your life, your thoughts, and your emotions; you may have a headache, feel shaky, nauseous, cold, confused, or exhausted. These withdrawal symptoms are similar to those that accompany withdrawal from other drugs. For hints on handling sugar withdrawal see pages 68 and 69.

If, after three to seven days, your cravings ease, and after three weeks they nearly cease; if you feel calmer, more energetic and clear-headed, your body is confirming your addiction to a harmful substance. The chemical on which you are dependent—your "drug of choice"—is sugar and/or white flour. If you notice no difference, feel no better, you have probably proved you are not a sugar addict.

JUNE'S STORY

Is it worth going through a few weeks of discomfort for a lifetime of improved health? June, another recovering sugar addict, thinks so. After a binge on sweets that left her quite ill, June decided to kick the habit entirely, to eliminate sugar and refined starches from her diet. Although she joined a support group for help, her recovery was not easy.

"My withdrawal was intense and very difficult," June recalls. "My cravings were constant. The first week, I had stomach-aches, headaches, frequent tears, weak knees, and I felt angry much of the time. For three weeks I noticed every ad for sweets, every candy display in the store. It seemed that all around me, people were snacking on delicious and wonderful things.

But as she stuck with her decision, June noticed, "I felt better, much healthier. But what astonished me was my increase in energy. I felt calm, fairly easygoing instead of irritable and depressed. It was easier to lose weight, since my horrible cravings to devour everything in sight were gone. My head was clearer, my brain seemed to work better. In fact, I was perking along so nicely, I was even beginning to be creative or productive in areas in which I had previously felt inadequate. My migraines disappeared, and my arthritic joints stopped creaking, swelling, and stiffening. Relationships that I had seriously questioned and in which I was feeling dissatisfied now seemed comfortable. I couldn't understand why I had been so dissatisfied with people I cared about."

"After that, I no longer desired sweets. I rarely missed what I had always thought of as my goodies in life. It wasn't even difficult anymore."

In the final analysis, it doesn't matter that the FDA hasn't banned sugar or that most physicians counsel only diabetics about sugar use. It doesn't matter how well or how badly another person handles sugar. To quote an old Foodaholics' cliché, "The proof of the pudding is in the eating." All that really matters is what happens to *you* when you abuse sugar, and what happens to you when you stop abusing it.

NOTES

1. *Webster's New Collegiate Dictionary*. (New York: World Publishing Company).
2. John Yudkin, *Sweet and Dangerous*. (New York: Peter H. Wyden, Inc. 1972), p. 3.
3. David Reuben, *Everything You Always Wanted to Know About Nutrition*. (New York: Simon and Schuster, 1978), p. 170.
4. Based on information from "Too Much Sugar." *Consumer Report*, March, 1978, pp. 136–9.
5. "Sugar Content of Dry Cereals," (St. Paul, MN: Group Health Plan, Inc., 1979). Reproduced by permission of The Health Education Dept. of Group Health Plan, Inc.
6. From *Meganutrition* by Richard A. Kunin, M.D. Copyright © 1980 by Richard A. Kunin, M.D. Used with permission of McGraw-Hill Book Company, p. 120.
7. Stanton Peele, *How Much Is too Much?* (Englewood Cliffs, NJ: Prentice-Hall, 1981), pp. 5–7.
8. Kunin, *Meganutrition*, p. 121.
9. Kunin, *Meganutrition*, p. 122.
10. Emanuel Cheraskin, W.M. Ringsdorf, and Arline Brecher, *Psychodietetics*. (Briarcliff Manor, NY: Stein and Day, 1974), p. 174.
11. Richard A. Passwater, *Supernutrition*. (New York: Simon and Schuster, 1975), pp. 142–3.
12. Chris W. Lecos, "Sugar, How Sweet It Is—And Isn't." *FDA Consumer*, February, 1980.
13. Jane Brody, *Jane Brody's Nutrition Book*. (New York: W.W. Norton and Company, 1981), p. 130.
14. Cheraskin, *Psychodietetics*, pp. 45–47.
15. William J. Lederer, *Marital Choices*. (New York: W.W. Norton and Company, 1981), pp. 203–213, 225–227.
16. *Minneapolis Star and Tribune*, June 23, 1982.

4

Hypoglycemia

Hypoglycemia, also called low blood sugar or carbohydrate intolerance, is a disorder of the body chemistry. The type of hypoglycemia with which I am concerned here is *not* caused by tumor or other serious illness. I will focus on reactive or functional hypoglycemia, which results from the body's chronic overproduction of insulin in response to intake of sugar, refined starches, and chemicals which include caffeine, alcohol, and nicotine.

DIAGNOSIS

Incidence

Hypoglycemia is a physical condition that occurs commonly in our population. This biochemical imbalance is so often misdiagnosed, misunderstood, and mistreated that the public and most health care practitioners are unaware of how frequently it occurs. One study suggests nearly 50 percent of the population is hypoglycemic.[1] Certain populations have an even higher incidence. Alan H. Nittler, a nutrition-oriented physician, writes that in his practice, close to 80 percent of his patients are hypoglycemic.[2]

Similar, and even higher, percentages of hypoglycemia have been identified and documented at the following human service and health care facilities in Minneapolis: Chrysalis, a resource center for chemically dependent women; Health Recovery Associates and Nutrition and Chemical Wellness Institute, where alcoholism is treated nutritionally; and the Foodaholics' Treatment Center, where eating disorders are treated biochemically as well as psychologically.

Dr. Abram Hoffer, in his book *Orthomolecular Nutrition*, writes that almost all of the 500 alcoholics tested showed low blood sugar levels, as do two-thirds of the people who suffer from neuroses or depression. Therefore, he places the incidence of hypoglycemia at 35 to 50 percent of the general population, and places the blame squarely on diets of junk food.[3]

Fact or Fad?

Some members of the medical establishment have used the increasing incidence of the disease as "proof" that hypoglycemia is a fad, an emotional disturbance, or a disease of neurotic women. Saunders and Ross, in their book *Hypoglycemia: The Disease Your Doctor Won't Treat*, note: "It seems that it is now a *fad* to label hypoglycemia a fad disease."[4] It is a fad to ignore or discount the patient's questions, request for a glucose tolerance test, or the symptoms exhibited during the test. It is a fad to administer a test that is too short to be conclusive, or to interpret the results as negative unless they meet certain rigid specifications.[5] It is also a fad to recommend eating sweets as a cure for those symptoms, which is like telling an alcoholic to have a drink so he will feel better.

Medical practitioners who term hypoglycemia a fad fail to take into account that the increased incidence of the disease seems to correlate with our increased intake of refined sugars and starches.

Obstacles to Diagnosis and Treatment

In the traditional medical model, the patient complains of a bodily malfunction and the physician figures out how to fix it, whereas in treating hypoglycemia, the primary responsibility lies with the patient. Not only does diagnosing hypoglycemia call for astuteness and sophistication on the physician's part, but also the hypoglycemic person has to be in charge of his/her treatment: monitoring symptoms, noticing the consequences of eating specific foods, and learning to trust body signals.

This nutritional rather than medical orientation puts physicians at a disadvantage, according to Saunders and Ross:

> The problem is that there are so few doctors today who know the first thing about nutrition, and few of them even have the desire to learn. They feel if something wasn't included in their limited training course on nutrition in medical school, it must not be very important. It is equally unfortunate that only 5 percent of our doctors know how to read or interpret the results of the glucose tolerance test when it is given, and some don't know how to treat hypoglycemia when it does show up on the tests.[6]

It follows that when we ask most physicians to deal with hypoglycemia, we not only challenge them to prescribe treatment in the unfamiliar area of nutrition, but we also challenge them to overcome their tendency to take control and expect patients to passively follow directions. Turning to the average nutritionist may not be very helpful, either.

Dr. Hoffer terms academic nutritionists "fossilized in their thinking at the 1950 level . . . The most advanced understanding of clinical nutrition is held by a few far-seeing clinicians and biochemists."[7] Traditional nutrition information is directed to people with normal nutritional requirements, not to individuals with specific nutritional requirements. Few health care professionals diagnose or know how to compensate nutritionally for physical problems caused by prolonged food or alcohol abuse. Some hypoglycemics absorb nutrients poorly. Therefore they require many times the Recommended Daily Allowance of some vitamins, food supplements, and basic nutrients.

Symptoms

Diagnosis of hypoglycemia is further complicated by the fact that symptoms vary, and often mimic or aggravate other health problems. The Adrenal Metabolic Research Society has published a list of symptoms or conditions in which hypoglycemia may play an important part:

Addiction
Alcoholism
Allergies

Antisocial behavior
Arthritis
Constant worries and anxiety
Convulsions
Depression
Fatigue and exhaustion
High-IQ youngsters labeled as underachievers
Incoordination
Inner trembling
Insomnia (wake up, can't go back to sleep)
Irritability
Juvenile delinquency
Leg cramps
Menière's disease
Nervous breakdown
Palpitations and tachycardia (noticeable heart action)
Phobias
Premenstrual tension
Migraine headaches
Frequent nightmares
Schizophrenia
Suicidal thoughts
Staggering
Ulcer-like pains
Tremors and cold sweats
Weakness and light-headedness, with or without fainting.[8]

An Emotional Disorder

It is obvious that symptoms of hypoglycemia manifest themselves both physically and psychologically. Depression, anxiety, a sense of foreboding, phobias, irritability, and negativity are common and are hazardous to relationships and achievements. Lack of energy, the most common physical complaint of people with hypoglycemia, is often misinterpreted as indicating emotional depression. Some of our clients have been misdiagnosed as having psychological problems instead of hypoglycemia. A few have even had electroconvulsive treatment.

There is a grain of truth in calling hypoglycemia an emotional disorder. Anger, sadness, and fear are all heightened by a hypoglycemic reaction. A momentary worry about having forgotten something can turn into sheer panic.

The fatigue and chronic low-energy commonly experienced by the hypoglycemic may, in time, result in a lack of motivation, leading to lowered self-esteem and serious depression. The hypoglycemic turns to sugar both for comfort and energy, setting up a conflicting, downward emotional spiral.

Trish's Story

When Trish gave up sugar, she regained her confidence. After three weeks on the hypoglycemic diet, Trish confided to her Foodaholics' group that she had become more assertive. She had been vaguely aware that her husband was juggling the finances in their jointly-owned business. In her sugar-induced depression, she had been sure she could do nothing about her anxiety, although her negative feelings were harming her marriage.

Trish noticed immediately how uneasy she felt without the aid of sugary sedatives. She told her husband of her need to have complete and accurate information about their finances, even if it meant facing unpleasant facts and lifestyle changes. Clearer thinking and a higher energy level helped Trish find a workable solution. She asked her husband to gather the figures for the accountant whom Trish then hired to check the books on a regular basis. Trish shared with the group her enthusiasm and delight with herself for "finally taking charge of my life."

As Trish's case shows, emotions are related to body chemistry. But calling hypoglycemia an emotional disorder is too simple. Functional or reactive hypoglycemia is really a nutritional or biochemical disorder, triggered in many people by abusive use of sugar, refined starches, alcohol, caffeine, or nicotine.

Hypoglycemia Pre-Test

This brief test, developed by Denver physician Dr. John F. Bumpus, is a tool designed to help you determine whether or not you might have hypoglycemia.[9]

Read each symptom listed and, if you suffer from it in any way, indicate the relative severity of your symptom with the following numbers: 1—mild symptoms; 2—moderate symptoms; 3—severe symptoms.

Total your score, leaving blanks for those symptoms which you do not experience at all.

Health Appraisal Indicator

1. _____ Abnormal craving for sweets
2. _____ Afternoon headaches
3. _____ Alcohol consumption
4. _____ Allergies—tendency to asthma, hay fever, skin rash, etc.
5. _____ Awaken after a few hours' sleep/hard to get to sleep
6. _____ Aware of breathing heavily
7. _____ Bad dreams
8. _____ Blurred vision
9. _____ Bleeding gums
10. _____ Brown spots or bronzing of skin
11. _____ Bruising easily (black-and-blue spots)
12. _____ "Butterfly" stomach, cramps
13. _____ Inability to make decisions easily
14. _____ Inability to start in A.M. before coffee
15. _____ Inability to work under pressure
16. _____ Chronic fatigue
17. _____ Chronic nervous exhaustion
18. _____ Convulsions
19. _____ Cravings for candy or coffee in the afternoons
20. _____ Crying easily for no reason
21. _____ Depression
22. _____ Dizziness
23. _____ Drinking _____ cups of coffee daily

24.	_____	Eating when nervous
25.	_____	Eating often or getting hunger pains or faintness
26.	_____	Faintness if meals delayed
27.	_____	Fatigue, relieved by eating
28.	_____	Fearfulness
29.	_____	Getting "shaky" if hungry
30.	_____	Hallucinations
31.	_____	Hand tremor
32.	_____	Heart palpitations if meals missed or delayed
33.	_____	Highly emotional
34.	_____	Hunger between meals
35.	_____	Insomnia
36.	_____	Inward trembling
37.	_____	Irritability before meals
38.	_____	Lacking energy
39.	_____	Magnifying insignificant events
40.	_____	Moods of depression, "blues," or melancholy
41.	_____	Poor memory
42.	_____	Reduced initiative
43.	_____	Sleepiness after meals
44.	_____	Sleepiness during day
45.	_____	Weakness, dizziness
46.	_____	Worrying, feeling insecure
47.	_____	Symptoms appearing before breakfast? (answer yes or no)
48.	_____	Feeling better after breakfast than before? (answer yes or no)

Total _____

"Some symptoms are more diagnostic than others. Answering any three of the following questions, 16, 17, 25, 26, 27, 29, 43, or 44, indicates you are likely to be suffering at least *some* sugar intolerance."[10] So, too, does a score greater than 40. If, on the basis of your test score, you decide to seek nutrition counseling or a Glucose Tolerance Test (GTT), it is important that you select someone who is expert in this area. Appendix A contains more information about the GTT.

TREATMENT

Jill's Story

Jill learned that she had to take charge of her life and her food when a hypoglycemic version of "The Lost Weekend" brought her face-to-face with her condition. Even though Jill was on one of her many diets, she had a craving for raisin pie. She fought her cravings for a time, and finally gave into them. Jill reasoned that if she had only pie and coffee for lunch, the calorie count wouldn't be too forbidding and she could work it off by running several errands.

Jill enjoyed every morsel of the pie. She even convinced herself that it was a healthy "meal"—after all, raisins are fruit, and they're loaded with iron.

She left the restaurant and started running errands. But she felt more and more sleepy. Visions of a nap kept her from concentrating. She felt irritable. "Poor me," she said to herself, "how come I never get to enjoy my time off? I shouldn't have to do all this dashing around."

Climbing a flight of stairs to a second-floor shop was a dreadful chore. Jill was puffing after about 20 stairs. Her problem wasn't only the stairs; just walking around seemed more difficult. Jill felt as though she weighed 300 pounds, not 140. She quit running errands and went home to nap. It didn't help much. She felt terrible.

Jill's illness forced her to take stock. She acknowledged that she had been feeling less and less well, that she had been having many less dramatic but similar experiences recently, and that she had been eating very poorly. Realizing the extent of her self destructiveness had a tremendous impact on Jill. She threw all the junk food out of her house to avoid temptation, and joined the Foodaholics' seminars and therapy group for motivation, support, and help in changing her destructive habits and thinking patterns.

A few weeks later, Jill confided to the group, "I feel much healthier when I *eat* healthy. I *knew* that my life was stressful. With a couple of teenagers and a high-pressure job, it continues to be stressful. But, without all that junk food to confuse, tire and stress me further, I seem to cope well most of the time. I don't feel nearly as pressured. Gradually, I am becoming addicted to feeling well and treating myself well. I'm very reluctant to sacrifice those good feelings just for some crummy food!"

Jill's decision to change lifestyles also affected her children. "I'm no longer willing to supply their 'drugs' either." Her teenagers were aghast, and did continue to "junk it up" at school and parties. Nevertheless, Jill had cause for celebration after a few weeks: "We don't have nearly as many quarrels now." She had not realized that eating sugary and starchy junk food had shortened tempers in her family.

Several months later Jill requested a six-hour Glucose Tolerance Test during a routine physical examination. To get an accurate interpretation of this test, Jill took a copy of her blood sugar curve to a nutritionist experienced in the diagnosis and treatment of hypoglycemia. The test clearly confirmed what Jill had suspected: She is hypoglycemic.

Nutrition Therapy:
the Hypoglycemic's Diet

The diet for hypoglycemia, which Jill began to follow long before her condition was officially diagnosed, is moderately high in protein and stresses complex natural carbohydrates. Unlike the poorly tolerated simple or refined carbohydrates, complex natural carbohydrates are absorbed slowly, and therefore do not cause a rapid increase in blood sugar levels.

The glucose metabolism is also taxed by large amounts of food at any one time. An eating plan which includes six small meals per day helps maintain a moderate blood sugar level for hypoglycemics like Jill.

The Suggested Food Plan for hypoglycemics offers a sound nutritional basis on which to design your own Healthy Eating Program. It is not a "prescription" for individuals, although the plan benefits many Foodaholics. Rather, tailor your program to your needs. Begin by adding your binge foods to the Foods to Avoid list. Then circle your favorite foods on the Recommended Foods list. In the process of creating your menu, include plenty of your favorite foods. If your cholesterol level is high, eat fewer servings of eggs, cheese, butter, meat, and nuts. If you have high blood pressure, limit your salt intake.

TABLE 4-1
SUGGESTED FOOD PLAN FOR HYPOGLYCEMICS

BREAKFAST:	*LUNCH:*	*DINNER:*
protein or dairy	protein	protein
whole grain	vegetables	vegetables
fruit	fruit	fruit
SNACK:	nuts/seeds	grain
fruit or vegetables	*SNACK:*	*SNACK:*
with nuts/seeds	fruit and/or	grain
or dairy	nuts/seeds	dairy or nuts/seeds

TABLE 4-2
RECOMMENDED FOODS

FRUIT	*NUTS*
fresh	almonds
frozen	walnuts
canned } unsweetened	hazelnuts
juice	pecans
VEGETABLES	*SEEDS*
fresh	pumpkin
frozen (no additives)	sesame
WHOLE GRAINS	sunflower
7-grain bread	poppy
soya bread	flax
cooked whole-grain cereal	*LEGUMES*
oats	peanuts
wheat	split peas
buckwheat	lentils
millet	garbanzo beans
bran	kidney beans
cornmeal	other beans
brown rice	

TABLE 4-2 (continued)

PROTEIN

   nuts/seeds

   soy meat substitute

   fish

   fowl

   eggs

   meat

   tofu

DAIRY

   yogurt

   cottage cheese

   milk

   cheese

FATS

   nut butter

   butter

   sesame seed oil

SALAD DRESSINGS

   Roquefort

   blue cheese

   vinegar and oil

   others (read labels)

ADDITIONAL POINTERS

— Cereal or pudding can be made with brown rice and/or millet. Add grains and seeds to taste. Cinnamon, nutmeg, carob powder, or vanilla can be added for flavoring. Leftovers make good snacks.

— Grains and legumes combined in a 2:1 ratio provide a complete protein.

— One meal of vegetables, steamed or in a salad, is advisable. Top with grated cheese, egg, or garbanzo beans.

— Use fruit juice and red meat sparingly.

— Fruit juice is best when diluted with equal amounts of spring water.

— Eat only protein breads: soya, sunflower, bran, stone-ground whole wheat, or other whole grains.

— Do not eat more than one slice of bread per meal (total of three per day).

— For other hints on making your hypoglycemic diet palatable and pleasurable, read Chapter 9 of Carlton Fredericks' book, *Low Blood Sugar and You.*[11]

TABLE 4-3
FOODS TO AVOID

BEVERAGES

alcoholic beverages
caffeine:
  cocoa
  coffee
  cola
  strong tea
grape juice
Ovaltine
Postum
prune juice
soft drinks

VEGETABLES

barley
potato chips or fries
white rice
sweet pickles
sweet relishes
sweet potatoes
yams

FRUIT

dried fruits
fruits canned in syrup

MEAT

*canned meats
*cold cuts
*hot dogs
*salami
*sausages
*scrapple

BREADS

avoid white flour
dry cereal
grits
hominy
matzo
pancakes
pizza
rolls
waffles
white bread
white crackers

PASTA

all pastas
noodles
matzo meal

MISCELLANEOUS

cashews
catsup
chestnuts
chewing gum
chili sauce
sweet and sour sauces
most canned soups
(read labels)
French dressing

TABLE 4-3 (continued)

DESSERTS	SUGARS**
cake	cane sugar
chocolate	refined sugar
cookies	raw sugar
custard	invert sugar
dessert topping	turbinado sugar
ice cream	brown sugar
jello	confectioners' sugar
pastry	sucrose
pie	glucose
pretzels	fructose
puddings	galactose
SWEETS**	dextrose
	levulose
candy	lactose
jam	maltose
jelly	dextrin
malt	corn syrup
marmalade	corn sugar
	maple syrup
	maple sugar
	honey
	molasses
	sorbitol
	manitol
	hexitol

*May have sugar as a preservative. Check labels.

**If a label lists several forms of sugar, add them together for total sugar content.

In order to achieve and maintain optimal weight and blood sugar levels, eliminate gravies, sauces, most salad dressings, as well as fried and breaded foods. Most of these items contain sugar or white flour and can be addictive. By overstimulating then numbing your tastebuds, these food items are likely to prevent you from fully experiencing the pleasurable taste of whole foods.

NUTRITIONAL SUPPLEMENTS

In addition to eating highly nutritious foods, some people benefit from megadoses of vitamins and minerals, prescribed after testing and diagnosis by an orthomolecular physician or nutritionist. Dr. Harvey M. Ross, president of the International College of Applied Nutrition, describes the supplemental program he often prescribes:

> In addition to recommending the proper diet, I give my patients supplements of natural B vitamins. The best B supplement is a B-complex tablet that has at least 50 mg. of all known natural B vitamins. This can be taken two or three times a day after meals. The B vitamins are very important in the chemical processes that are involved in the utilization of carbohydrates. A few patients I have seen did not improve until the B vitamins were added. In addition to the B vitamins I usually order at least 1,000 mg. of natural vitamin C and 400 units of natural vitamin E twice a day after meals, for general health.[12]

COPING WITH WITHDRAWAL

Alcohol, drugs, narcotics, nicotine, and caffeine are taboo for the hypoglycemic. When you eliminate sugar, caffeine, and nicotine, you may temporarily experience withdrawal symptoms. You may choose to eliminate these chemicals one at a time. As you steadily progress, becoming emotionally, physically and mentally healthier, you will be more attuned to the symptoms caused by any remaining addictions. Eliminating them will become a sought-after goal, rather than a deprivation.

Another method of coping with addictions, particularly all of those that create a hypoglycemic reaction, is to handle them simultaneously—cold turkey! You will go through the pangs of withdrawal only once. Your total withdrawal time will be shorter.

Whichever method you use, you will handle withdrawal symptoms better if you carefully plan other self-indulgences while abstaining from your addictive chemical(s). Nurture yourself. Spend time with people who will be kind to you or who will take care of you. Put yourself in a nurturing environment—a cabin in the woods, near the water, anywhere you feel happy and peaceful. Realize that this transition, like all transitions, will be stressful, and decide the way you can manage it best. You may choose to immerse yourself in work, vacation, or visit friends. During withdrawal, allow yourself frequent protein snacks rather than trying at first to lose weight. Dr. Ross's recommendations for supplements (page 68) also help ease withdrawal.

Read Chapters 10-14 for good healthful alternatives that you can introduce to your life, so that your beloved, but abusive, substances will become less important.

CHARTING YOUR PROGRESS

Recording changes in eating patterns, emotional states, and coping skills can be useful. Keep general notes on what types of foods you do and do not eat, noting how you feel emotionally and physically. Writing entries at least two to three times weekly in a diary or journal will enable you to count your successes and avoid fooling yourself.

I added small amounts of dried fruit to my diet for a while, and told myself I was feeling fine. Since I am very fond of these foods, I managed to kid myself for about a month. Then a review of my journal revealed that I had sabotaged my high energy level and compromised my easygoing emotional state. In fact, I was feeling rather unwell, but had gradually grown used to it.

A journal can keep us from accepting as a normal condition feeling under par. A journal is useful when we scold ourselves for not being perfect or for our failure to adhere to an ideal eating program. Comparing our earlier entries with our current status may point out our considerable progress.

Generally speaking, people who have hypoglycemia are "allergic" to blood-sugar raising chemicals such as sugar, refined flour, caffeine, nicotine, and alcohol. Other food allergies are explored in the next chapter, Hidden Addictions: Food Allergies.

NOTES

1. *Hypoglycemia and Me*? (Troy, NY: Adrenal Metabolic Research Society of the Hypoglycemia Foundation, Inc., 1973), p. 27.
2. Alan H. Nittler, *Hypoglycemia (Low Blood Sugar)*. (Monrovia, CA: The National Health Federation).

3. Abram Hoffer, *Orthomolecular Nutrition*. (New Canaan, CN: Keats Publishing, 1978), p. 20.

4. From *Hypoglycemia: The Disease Your Doctor Won't Treat*, by Jeraldine Saunders and Harvey M. Ross, M.D., pp. 25–27. Copyright © 1980 by Jeraldine Saunders and Harvey M. Ross, M.D. Reprinted by arrangement with Pinnacle Books, Inc., New York, NY.

5. *Ibid.*

6. *Ibid.*, p. 147.

7. Hoffer, *Orthomolecular Nutrition*, p. 5.

8. *Hypoglycemia and Me?*, pp. 4–5.

9. Copyright © 1974 by E. Cheraskin, W.M. Ringsdorf, Jr., and Arline Brecher. From the book *Psychodietetics*, pp. 79–80. Reprinted with permission of Stein and Day Publishers and McIntosh and Otis, Inc.

10. *Ibid.*, p. 80.

11. Carlton Fredericks, *Low Blood Sugar and You*. (New York: Grosset and Dunlap Company, 1969), pp. 142–152.

12. Saunders and Ross, *Hypoglycemia*, pp. 73–74.

5

Hidden Addictions: Food Allergies

The word "allergy" is familiar to us. We might have a common allergy ourselves or know someone who is allergic to pollen, strawberries, seafood, or penicillin. An allergy is an intolerance for, or sensitivity to, a certain substance. This intolerance or sensitivity manifests itself in many ways, including these rather common physical reactions: watery eyes, skin rash, hives, blocked nasal passages, general or localized itching. Although I share the growing concern regarding allergic reactions to chemicals we are exposed to daily (sprays, preservatives and dyes), I will focus here exclusively on food allergies and related implications for the compulsive eater.

Most of us have a self-diagnosed food allergy/sensitivity, whether we call it that or not. A certain food irritates our stomach or skin, so we avoid it. We don't need medical assistance to identify the cause of the problem. We use trial and error to find the culprit And, we usually don't need advice or encouragement to eliminate it.

Allergies are, by nature, *idiopathic:* Each person has a different experience. A substance which produces an allergic reaction in me may not affect you at all, or the substance that causes a rash on my skin may cause a pain in your stomach or a feeling of anxiety and fear in someone else. Allergies are caused by a malfunctioning of the body's immune system.

The inflammation that signals an allergic reaction can appear anywhere in or on the body. An allergy can produce an astonishing array of symptoms. Food allergies can affect us in three ways: physically, perceptually, and emotionally. Physically, they can cause rashes, headaches, pains, or a multitude of bodily ills. Perceptually, they can distort what we see and hear, and this affects our reading, writing, and ability to concentrate. Emotionally, they can cause feelings of anger, impatience, depression, fear, or temporary euphoria.

ALLERGY AND ADDICTION: CAUSE AND EFFECT

To understand food allergy, consider the process of addiction. Initially, we enjoy a food/substance and become accustomed to it (build tolerance). We probably are unaware of our subtle negative physical reactions and unlikely to relate these changes to the food we are eating. Eating the offending food hides or "masks" these allergic symptoms, so we develop a need for the food (dependence) in order to stave off such symptoms. Ironically, the very food that is causing our problem is the substance that alleviates our symptoms, somewhat like an alcoholic relieving the shakes with a morning drink.

Although we can reduce or mask our symptoms by frequent "fixes" of the allergic substance, they are always present at a low-grade level. The symptoms may become more severe with time, requiring more of the allergen to mask them and thus increase our cravings. Meanwhile, we food "addicts" are living with chronic, low-level illness, and we may also be risking development of serious health problems associated with poor nutrition and overeating.

This allergic/addictive relationship can account for the Foodaholic's loss of control and obsession with certain types of food. Ruth was "hooked" on peanuts. It seemed as if they controlled her. She thought she could neither stop nor get enough of them. After removing the peanuts from her diet and passing through some initial withdrawal symptoms, she felt little desire for them—until she tried a few and began eating them compulsively again.

Michael's Story

Michael found out about his food addiction durii
treatment. He had already completed Foodaholi
fied many of the psychological factors in his f(
less destructively, but still had a tendency to bir
kinesiologic testing (described in Appendix B)
reactions to several food substances. Water (sp
coffee, sugar, and salt produced no reaction. Bu
baking powder—turned his muscles to spaghetti!

Michael wasn't aware of problems caused by his allergy, but the results of the test were so dramatic that he decided to experiment with a sulfur-free diet. It wasn't easy—sulfur is a common preservative used in hundreds of food items, things as diverse as dried fruit, wine, bread, and beer.

Michael had rarely included ice cream with his groceries because he would eat it all and still want more. He discovered that selecting ice cream sweetened with cane sugar rather than sulfurous corn syrup enabled him to eat a dishful and then forget about it! After eliminating sulfur from his diet, Michael experienced fewer mood swings, more energy, and reduced cravings. Even though sulfur-free eating was restricting, it was also freeing to Michael.

DIAGNOSIS AND TREATMENT

The following steps may help you to discover what food allergies/addictions you may have:

Step I: Educate Yourself

You can read more extensively on allergy by referring to sources used in this chapter and Appendix B. These materials offer detailed information on allergy and provide a variety of professional opinions on all aspects of food and chemical allergies. Becoming well informed is an important first step in assuming responsibility for your own health care.

Talk with people who will share some of their experiences in changing diet to treat food allergies. Establish a support system which will encourage you to further explore your food sensitivities. Clinical Ecology

...g new field of medicine that is worthy of your attention. ...ical specialization is based on a belief that many mental and ...al symptoms or dysfunctions are caused by environmental fac-...s such as food allergies and sensitivities to chemicals.

Step II: Test Yourself

Since we are often addicted to the foods to which we are allergic, the first place to look for allergies is in the foods you crave and eat most often. Dr. Mackarness, author of *Eating Dangerously: The Hazards of Hidden Allergy,*[1] suggests that you make a list of everything you eat at least every three days. Look at your list and identify those foods you crave, the ones you binge on. If there are several such foods, do they share a common factor? If you binge on ice cream, yogurt, and cheese, for example, milk may be the allergen. If you stuff on rolls and pasta, you may have an allergy to wheat. If you suspect a specific food, eliminate it from your diet completely for five days.

The usual culprits are the most commonly eaten foods. Clinical ecologist Dr. Theron Randolph includes the following foods among those which produce a high incidence of allergies in North America: coffee, corn, wheat, milk, eggs, yeast, beef, and pork.[2]

Note your reactions in your food diary. Are you beginning to experience withdrawal symptoms on or about day three? Do you feel a distinct improvement, physically and mentally, by day five? If withdrawal symptoms, followed by improvement represents your pattern of reaction, chances are you've found your allergen. For confirmation, try some of the suspect substance on day six and see how you react.

Better yet, allow at least a month for your body to clear the substance and then experiment. The reaction, now unmasked, will usually be fast and powerful. Michael discovered this by accident when, after a long period of sulfur-free eating, he tasted a cherry crepe. The sauce obviously contained sulfurous cornstarch because the first bite literally took Michael's breath away, and a tingly numbness spread down into his arms and hands. Needless to say, Michael did not finish his dessert. He dramatically confirmed the necessity for his sulfur-free diet. (Note: If you find yourself in the midst of an allergic reaction and do not suffer from hypertension, simply dissolve a little baking soda in water and drink it to help relieve some of the symptoms.)

You can perform a variety of food tolerance tests on your own or with help from a food therapy program or professional. You may need to experiment with different testing methods and observe your reactions to these methods just as you observe your reactions to the different foods you eat. Additional self-testing procedures appear in Appendix B.

If you are allergic to more than one substance, or to an additive, such as sulfur, which appears in many foods, more sophisticated testing may be required. When seeking a professional to verify your findings or to assist in allergy testing, carefully select an orthomolecular physician or nutritionist, a chiropractor extensively trained in applied kinesiology, or a clinical ecologist who is familiar with the work of Drs. Theron Randolph, Herbert Rinkel, Carlton Lee, and Marshall Mandell. A personal referral is a good method for selecting this individual, as is limiting your choices to specialists who perform "provocative" tests by ingestion, inhalation, injections, or extracts on or under the tongue.[3] Names and addresses of groups and publications dedicated to education and research on food allergies and chemical intolerances are listed in the book *Coping With Your Allergies* by Natalie Golos and Frances Golos Golbitz.[4]

Step III: Heal Yourself

I invite you to remember that it took years for you to develop and sustain your food allergies. Allow yourself some time to give them up mentally and physically and to clear the allergens out of your system and life-style.

A *fixed* allergy is one which consistently causes a reaction. This means that every time you eat this food you will have a reaction. The healthful choice is to eliminate this food from your diet. Fifty to 90 percent of all food allergies are *cyclic*. Cyclic allergies are intermittent and depend on how often and how much you eat of a specific food.[5] Experiment with avoiding the offending foods for a few weeks or months, and you may acquire a tolerance for them. You may never be able to eat them in the consistent fashion that fostered your addiction, but with proper treatment, you may not have to eliminate these foods totally from your diet.

The Rotary Diversified (RD) Diet, developed by Dr. Herbert J. Rinkel in 1934, is the basis of the treatment diet for food allergy offered by many clinical ecologists. Dr. Theron Randolph in his book, *An Alter-*

native Approach to Allergies, describes the rules he uses in devising an individual diet for allergy patients.

Rule 1   Eat whole, unadulterated foods.

Rule 2   Diversify your diet—expand, explore . . .

Rule 3   Rotate your diet. Eat a particular food only once every five days. This pattern will help you to avoid dependence and the possible development of an allergic reaction to previously nontoxic foods.

Rule 4   Rotate food families. To avoid a cross-reaction to the "relatives" of a food you are allergic to, rotate food family members every two days.

Rule 5   Eat only foods to which you are not allergic at first. After a period of avoidance, you may regain tolerance to troublesome foods.[6]

For a more complete explanation of this diet, refer to these books: *An Alternative Approach to Allergies* or *Coping With Your Allergies.*

The benefits of the RD diet are many. It helps to pinpoint present allergies. It helps in developing and maintaining a tolerance for past allergens. It protects you from developing other food allergies by overexposure to certain foods. It helps a Foodaholic avoid psychological as well as physical dependence.

After Howard discovered his wheat allergy, he substituted brown rice for bread. Soon he was experiencing an allergic reaction to rice. After several months on the RD diet he finds he can now eat rice on a rotating basis and is beginning to experiment with eating wheat to see if it is a fixed or cyclic allergen for him. Howard was motivated to explore the possibility of allergies because of his headaches, sleep disturbance, floating anxiety, and increasing depression unrelated to specific life events. After several months on the RD diet Howard felt "wonderful . . . little depression. Life feels more manageable . . . I deal with stress better."

Being aware of your body's reactions is the most important aspect of treating an allergy. The main issue in being responsible for your own health care is learning to make positive choices to take better care of yourself. For people with allergies, as for hypoglycemics, stress sets off food intolerances because the release of adrenalin stimulates the fight against the toxic substance. So monitor your food intake carefully during busy or emotionally charged times.

Mahatma Ghandi once stated: "Only give up a thing when you want some condition so much that the thing has no longer any attraction for you, or when it seems to interfere with that which is more greatly desired."[7] Ruth and Howard both realized that their allergies were interfering with the higher level of health they desired. They became willing to give up eating their favorite foods for the greater goal of improved health and well-being. When we make such a choice consciously and freely, we do not feel victimized by our allergies. Renouncing the offending food, then, is not a sacrifice, but a positive alternative.

NOTES

1. Dr. Richard Mackarness, *Eating Dangerously: The Hazards of Hidden Allergy* (New York: Harcourt Brace and Jovanovich, 1976).
2. Theron G. Randolph, M.D., and Ralph W. Moss, Ph.D., *An Alternative Approach to Allergies*. (New York: Lippincott and Crowell, 1980), p. 20.
3. Dr. Marshall Mandell and Lynne Waller Scanlon, *Dr. Mandell's 5-Day Allergy Relief System*. (New York: Thomas Y. Crowell Company, 1979), p. 17.
4. Natalie Golos and Frances Golos Golbitz with Frances Spatz Leighton, *Coping With Your Allergies*. (New York: Simon and Schuster, 1979), pp. 332–334.
5. Mandell, *Allergy Relief System*, p. 263.
6. Randolph, *Alternative Approach*, pp. 179–182.
7. Louis Fisher, *Ghandi, His Life and Messages For The World*. (New York: Mentor Books, 1960), p. 34.

III
THE FOODAHOLIC
WAY OF LIFE

6

The Foodaholic
Family System

Not long ago, I observed the care and feeding of a future Foodaholic. I was with a small group of people, soaking up the Fall sunshine around the swimming pool of a northern Minnesota resort. Nearby sat a young mother and her six-month-old daughter—I'll call the baby Julie for the purpose of this story. It was evident that Julie was an extremely alert and active child. She squirmed in her mother's lap, pumping and waving her plump little arms and legs.

INTRUSIVENESS
AND BATTLE FOR CONTROL

Mother proceeded to push Julie into a reclining position, and put the bottle into her mouth. The child half-heartedly pulled at the nipple for a few minutes, then batted it away and sat up to look around again. This push-pull sequence between mother and daughter was repeated until the child had completely emptied her bottle.

Julie's mother doesn't seem to trust Julie to be aware of and to act upon her food needs. Mother determines when and how much Julie eats. Mother fails to respond to Julie's need to explore rather than to eat. Julie's mother acts out of her own needs to control and play the Good Mother Role. Such intrusive parenting has been termed narcissistic[1] and crazymaking.[2] A parent who thinks or acts for a child may cause the child to question or ignore his/her own feelings and needs.

Like a typical Foodaholic, Julie is learning to eat or stop eating according to external cues such as her mother's behavior or the quantity of food available. She may already be denying her body's cues.

Given this form of parental behavior, it is likely that when Julie reaches toilet-training age (or even before), Mother may become as involved with Julie's elimination as she is now with her consumption. At that time, should Julie fail to produce on the toilet, thus showing she is in charge of her own process, Mother could escalate her efforts to control, resorting to enemas and suppositories. This scenario is not farfetched considering that Julie and her mother are already engaged in a battle over who will control Julie's body.

When the nurturer-child relationship regarding food develops as has Julie's and her mother's, the child will not learn to be *accurately* hungry. It is not true that we all recognize our hunger and which foods we need to eat. One reason we have food problems is because we do not appropriately connect our honest sensation of hunger with food and with eating. We either did not learn good ways to respond to hunger in childhood or disconnected the idea of eating from hunger later in life.

Don's Story

Don confuses appetite and hunger. He does not allow himself to feel hungry; he just keeps eating. Don was surprised to learn that if he had eaten a satisfying meal, then he probably wouldn't be hungry only two hours later. "I needed that information. I could have eaten one breakfast, and if I saw a pan of rolls, I wouldn't have any idea of thinking or saying 'I'm not hungry.' If it looks good, I'm hungry. I've never learned to consider my physical feelings of hunger or fullness and my recent food consumption in my decision to eat."

Wanda's Story

Many Foodaholics can trace a noticeable change in their eating behavior to a specific event or time. Wanda acquired a consistently critical stepfather at the age of six. Prior to her mother's second marriage, Wanda had a healthy relationship with food. Snapshots of Wanda at age five and six show a rounded body—not chubby, but by no means lean or lanky either. When Stepdad teased Wanda about being fat, she reacted by becoming obsessed with food. At times she tried hard not to eat much and to deny her hunger, because Stepdad was always watching. But mostly she thought about and consumed food more and more. She gained weight steadily. Wanda disconnected her eating from her hunger during a difficult transition stage.

Young Julie, too, is well on her way to becoming a Foodaholic. She may learn to pay no attention to her body unless it is so stuffed that she feels uncomfortable. Hunger may be something she rarely experiences, because she either eats constantly or strictly by the clock. She may have little sense of hunger or fullness, limited knowledge of her likes and dislikes, and a blocked awareness of which foods feel good and which ones do not. She may begin to seek sweeter and more exotic substances to substitute for actually tasting her food and taking pleasure in the act of eating.

Julie may, at school-age, become confused by her mother's behavior. When she becomes six or twelve, Mother, and maybe Father and siblings as well, could begin to comment on Julie's body, her appearance. Julie's family may no longer be proud of their obviously well-fed child. They might be ashamed of chubby Julie. Mother will probably still be controlling what Julie eats, but instead of pushing food, she may be trying to *limit* Julie's intake.

FAMILY VALUES

Food Equals Love

Like many people who care for and about children, Julie's mother sincerely believes that her job as nurturer includes responsibility for getting food into her baby—at almost any cost. These nurturers offer food as evidence of their love and competence; they equate love with abundant and exciting foods offered frequently. Children assimilate these values and accept food as a symbol of love.

Consequently, both parent and child feel upset and confused when the emphasis switches to withholding food. If Mother later attempts to limit Julie's intake, she will find herself caught in a no-win situation. Since she has long been playing the Good Mother Role, instead of tuning in to Julie's needs and natural processes, she will then face a conflict between: "People will think I'm terrible; I have a fat child," and "I feel so guilty. I must not love my child. I'm taking some of her food away." Julie's mother may react to that conflict with inconsistent behavior toward her, creating a double-bind for the child with both "eat, eat, eat" and "you're too fat" messages.

Having learned to view food as an expression of love, Julie could feel abandoned when food is withheld. Maybe in Julie's family, food is the major or only expression of love. Adult Foodaholics who have adopted the value that food equals love may feel deprived when on a rigid, restricted diet. Old feelings of abandonment return and are aggravated by denial of perhaps the only form of self-love or self-care they will allow themselves.

(POOR BOUNDARIES)

Julie could grow up to be obsessed with food—the consumption or withholding of it. She may eat large quantities, and follow her binges with fasts, diets, or purges. She could feel out of control in her eating and her obsessing about food. Although her lack of control might surprise and dismay her, it is perfectly consistent with the way she has been raised. She has not been the one in control of her eating all her life. Mother has. Mother's behavior invites Julie not to grow up. The implied messages are: "Don't think (I will do your thinking for you); Don't feel (what you feel)";[3] and "You are not in charge of your body (I am)."

Children reared in Foodaholic families experience a strange mixture of helplessness and power. For instance, Julie's seven-year-old brother, Stuart, might lose his appetite during the summer heat, only to discover that his failure to eat can send the family into a real tailspin. He would then have a handy means of getting lots of attention.

Both very thin or plump adolescents may find that their parents make negative comments about appearance. Their siblings may well follow the parents' lead by teasing the teenager. As painful as these judgments may be, and as much as an adolescent's self-esteem may suffer from them, he or she may be using unacceptable appearance as a tool for rebellion.

Criticism of Appearance and Eating

Values about appearance and eating can be transmitted in very subtle ways. Samantha may hear her mother complain often about her *own* extra weight and how ugly and fat she is. Or maybe it's Dad who makes disapproving comments to Mom, and vice versa. In any event, Samantha matures in an environment where it is clearly not acceptable to have an ample body. Should her own body be pudgy for a time during childhood, or well-rounded during adolescence, she may decide that not only her appearance, but *she* is unacceptable. Starting from this approval-seeking, self-hating stance, she may begin a lifelong struggle with a diet-binge cycle, with her self-esteem dependent upon an unstable foundation of food intake and appearance.

After a time, we Foodaholics can maintain this struggle by ourselves even without hearing criticism. Like the rest of us, Julie can install her own personal Resident Critic in her head. (See Chapter 11). Then she may hear the put-down dialogue in her head no matter how positively people react to her. Or Julie may decide that it is natural and right for her appearance and food intake to be constantly evaluated, measured, and compared, and invite these criticisms.

Once Julie has become her own worst critic, she will be merciless with herself even while she is very understanding of the faults and short-comings of others. She can pick and snipe at herself, harangue and holler at every bulge, real or imagined, every deviation from the "perfect" model of appearance, food intake, or performance. She can easily give a five-minute running commentary on what is wrong with her body, and stutter and gulp when asked to reveal what she likes about her physical self.

Food is only one of the commodities she may devour or gobble up indiscriminately. She may also incorporate, unevaluated, the following: people's impression of her; others' opinions of what her role in life should be and their rules for her behavior; parents', peers', or hosts' ideas of what she should ingest; society's notions of how she should look; and the media portrayal of high-calorie junk food as desirable and fun.

LACK OF BOUNDARIES

Although often more subtle than described here, the ways in which Julie and her mother relate are typical in a Foodaholic family system. Julie and her mother do not relate to each other as separate people. They do not have clearly established boundaries which distinguish Julie's percep-tions, needs, and responsibilities from Mom's perceptions, needs, and responsibilities.

In a healthy family system, individuality is nurtured and differences are respected. Each person is recognized and respected for having territory, personality, thoughts, emotions, values, needs and wants, patterns of behavior, and appearance that are unique. Parents and other nurturers are sensitive and responsive to children's nonverbal signals, helping them become responsible for knowing what they need and skilled at getting those needs met.

In the highly enmeshed Foodaholic family system, often all mem-bers have blurred boundaries. It is never really clear just who is sad, who is tired, who is hungry, or what any one person thinks or feels. We "know" that our parent's unhappiness or dissatisfaction are "caused by" our be-havior, size, or food intake. Others imply, or we assume, that we are in charge of their happiness and responsible for their emotional well-being.

"MOM, HOW COME WHEN YOU'RE DIETING
YOU TRY TO FEED ME TWICE AS MUCH?"
(HE HAS CLEAR BOUNDARIES)

CARETAKING

Caretakers are people who spend time and energy figuring out and meeting the needs of others while neglecting their own self-care. In order to focus on others more effectively, caretakers frequently block their awareness of their own emotions or needs. As skillful as they are in doing for others, caretakers have little practice in taking action toward filling their own needs or wants. Their solitary or primary *self*-care skill is usually feeding themselves. When they feel depleted from giving so much of themselves to others, they typically use food to replenish.

Caretaker roles are often assumed early in life. Children who decide that they have the power and responsibility to keep one or both parents happy are engaging in magical thinking and role reversal. Instead of the parent becoming attuned to the child, and learning which cry or behavior might indicate pain, discomfort, hunger, fear, or boredom, the *child* becomes highly perceptive and sensitive to the parent's reactions, and may attempt to walk a tightrope of maintaining peace or happiness within the family.

Such a child may feel like a failure or decide that he or she is a bad person because it simply is not possible to make or keep other people happy. Often these children carry this same belief in their magical power into adulthood. They think their job in life is to keep others calm, content, sober, or married. Adults who grow up in such circumstances cannot comprehend that children are not *supposed* to have that kind of power or responsibility. We may feel appalled and disgusted with a sibling who feels free to play and be a child or who seems to be "inconsiderate" as an adult.

We Foodaholics face the confusion of double messages and our double bind once again as we conspire to fit into these roles. On one hand we let others do our thinking for us, set the standards for our eating and appearance, judge our every move. We "Don't Grow Up."[4] And contrarily, we think we must hurry up and grow up (Don't Be a Child[5]) in order to be like parents to our parent(s) or others, to keep them happy, "fix" their feelings, and be sensitive to their unspoken needs. Such confusion and stress is enough to "drive one to eat," or so we may tell ourselves.

CHEMOPHILIC THINKING

Quite simply, chemophilic thinking is the belief that whatever might be wrong, there is a substance available that will effect a cure or solve the problem. As food is used to help us solve problems, dull emotions, and cope with challenging situations, the underlying message becomes: "Don't feel. Don't think. Eat!"

This is the message when a child is fed every time she or he cries.

This is the message when a toddler falls down and is comforted with a cookie. This is the message when a child whines with boredom and is offered food for diversion. This is the message when two children fight over a toy, and one is offered candy as a pacifier. This is the message when a junior high youngster is distraught over a real or imagined rejection and gets sympathy in the form of a piece of cake. This is the message when a young person, tense with anxiety over a school test, is reassured and encouraged with food.

We may observe other examples of chemophilic thinking within the family system. We may hear someone who is tense being urged to take a drink, an aspirin, or a pill to relax. We may see tranquilizers shared among mourners of a dead relative. We may notice folks regularly using a couple of drinks each night to help them make the transition from a harried day. We may hear people say: "I need a drink" or "I need something sweet."

We may conclude that certain substances can make people feel better. The only problem seems to be to select the right substance for each troublesome situation. Since food is our "drug of choice," we continue our magical thinking that if we can only find the right food in the proper quantity, we will feel better.

In summary, the Foodaholic family system tends to be highly intrusive and enmeshed. The dynamics of this system can foster both an absence of personal boundaries and some distinct areas of conflict. Deciding who is responsible for whom and how far that responsibility extends is one problem. Another serious problem is the use and abuse of substances in order to avoid conflict or unpleasant emotions.

We have blurred boundaries in that we:

- Ignore our internal experience of satiation or hunger and allow external factors to determine what or how much we eat.
- Incorporate others' critical attitudes and fail to develop or to heed our own standards or values regarding food, appearance, and our roles in life.
- Fail to separate responsibility for ourselves from responsibility to others.
- Fail to recognize, accept, or act upon our own emotions.
- Fail to retain only our own emotions when relating to someone experiencing different emotions.

The areas of conflict or double binds are:

- We hear others say, and we tell ourselves, Eat, eat, eat, but don't get fat!
- Many of us have one or more persons in our lives who are domineering and attempt to control us (Don't Grow Up), but we may wishfully believe that if we take care of them just right, we can keep them happy (Hurry Up and Grow Up).
- We and/or others in our lives believe that food equals love, but, on the other hand, we think they'd love us more if we ate less. We may feel rejected or abandoned when we/they ration that "love."
- We may think we are helpless and lack power or control over our eating or our lives. Yet we have this magical power to be responsible for others: to fix their feelings, to solve their problems. If we don't take care of them, we fear something dreadful will happen to them. In this way, we believe we are mighty powerful!

(POOR BOUNDARIES!)

The Foodaholic family system is but one unit in the Foodaholic society. Both the family and society influence, and are influenced by the media.

NOTES

1. Alice Miller, *Prisoners of Childhood.* (New York: Basic Books, Inc., 1981), p. 8.
2. Dr. George R. Bach and Dr. Herb Goldberg, *Creative Aggression.* (New York: Doubleday and Company, Inc., 1974), pp. 69–76.
3. Robert Goulding and Mary Goulding, "Injunctions, Decisions and Redecisions." *Transactional Analysis Journal,* Vol. 6, No. 1, January, 1976.
4. *Ibid.*
5. *Ibid.*

7

Our Foodaholic Society and the Media

We are a society obsessed with both food and slender bodies. The media foster and reflect the double messages and our resulting conflict.

DOUBLE MESSAGES

Thin is In

No more than 5 percent of people cast in television programs or commercials are overweight, a poor representation for that 35 to 40 percent of the population. It seems that the more amply-fleshed performers are either highly talented, established stars, or they are the object of jokes and put-downs. Similar images prevail in most general-audience and women's magazines. In fact, women's bodies, as seen on television and in the magazines, often seem adolescent or anorexic. The message "Thin Is In" is further emphasized in the volume of advertising for weight reduction programs, diet pills, diet soft drinks, and yogurt.

Eat, Eat, Eat

Yet often a magazine which features half a dozen pages of their latest diet will devote many times that number of pages to food ads, elaborate high-calorie menus, recipes, and food preparation hints. On television, the food-slender body conflict is highlighted by the fact that the slender folks whom we see and are encouraged to resemble, are not likely to *stay* thin if they actually consume the products they promote. A high percentage of advertising on television and in the women's magazines focuses on food items, many of them high calorie and non-nutritional.

Food Is Love

In our culture we confuse love and food. Advertisers play on this confusion. They equate the offering of food with proving one's love, hospitality, or friendship.

- Nothin' says lovin' like something from the oven.
- Because she loves them, she buys brand Z.
- My children are special to me, so I give them a nutritious snack after school ___. (The first ingredient of this snack is sugar and several others are preservatives and artificial colorings; only one or two ingredients are real food.)
- To let them know you care, buy Brand X.
- Bake someone happy.
- Love is a bundt.
- Welcome him home with Green Giant.

Food Wins Friends

Robert T. Smith, columnist for the Minneapolis Tribune, offers this TV version of American values:

> The city kid comes to the farm to stay with his country cousin *all summer long*!
> It's a real blow to the farm kids. How can they deal with a city kid *all summer long*?
> Don't fret. The city kid whips out a pack of M&M candies, and he is immediately welcome and you just know there will be no trouble *all summer long.*

If you have some M&Ms, then you can easily win friends. No matter that you're a dunce, a dullard, and have bad breath. Such a thing taught to susceptible kids can be disastrous.[1]

Smith writes in another column:

This guy's having a great party at his pad, see. And there are all sorts of people there a-laughin' and a-hollerin'.
And then, it happens. He runs out of Doritos.
The party's over. There is silence. He offers other munchies, but no.
"It was a lovely party, Charlie," says an attractive young woman. All then leave.
Happens all the time, right? No, only in television commercials.
It's another example of how the TV ads teach us values. Without Doritos, how can there be friendship? Or fun?[2]

Because food takes on so many meanings in our society, our efforts to eat healthy substances in reasonable quantities may be threatening to others. They may try to sabotage us in their need to uphold society's values about food.

- You mean to tell me you aren't going to eat any when I made them especially for you?
- My dinner party is no time to cut corners. You can diet tomorrow.
- Party Pooper!
- I'm embarrassed. You insulted our hostess.
- A vacation is for lots of good eating. Now don't put a damper on it.
- Here I take you to this outstanding restaurant and you hardly eat at all.

PROMOTING FOOD ABUSE

Notice the many commercials that state or imply: "You'll want to eat more, and more, and more of our product." Food manufacturers are not social service agencies. They are in business for profit. Paul Stitt, author of *Fighting the Food Giants*, discovered while he was employed in the food industry that manufacturers use sugar, fat, and salt liberally because these ingredients make heavy contributions to the weight of the product *and* they stimulate the appetite. Sugar, fat, and salt have properties that arouse what he terms the "Can't Eat Just One Syndrome."[3]

"When will we face the fact that the sugar business thrives on an addiction encouraged in the ignorant or defenseless?" asks Dr. Richard Kunin, in his book *Meganutrition*.[4] As harsh as Dr. Kunin's words may seem, many of us who are recovering Foodaholics will claim we were "ignorant" of the price we were paying for our repeated junk food fixes and "defenseless" in the face of the cravings they spawned.

PROMOTING MAGICAL THINKING

When we complain we're bored, or that life is dull, we are reflecting our society's values that normal levels of activity or sensation are undesirable. Food is used as a sedative for any uncomfortable situation or emotion: anxiety, boredom, disappointment, or anger. We tend to fear the power of our emotions. We view our anger toward others as potentially annihilating, or our sadness as overwhelming. As a consequence, we do not allow ourselves to "feel" very often.[5] We have the chemophilic thinking described in the last chapter.

Learning Foodaholic thinking and non-feeling begins early in life. Perhaps when you were a small child, you heard statements such as these:

> *Parent:* I'm sorry you're having a bad day. You can have another piece of cake.
>
> *Teacher:* Too bad they don't want you on their team. Now forget about it and come help me set out the snacks. You may even take an extra cookie.
>
> *Doctor or Nurse:* That shot didn't hurt much, did it? Here's your lollipop for being so brave.

As an adult, you now hear these messages:

- Nervous? Take Compoz.
- Can't sleep? Take Sominex.
- Upset stomach? Take Alka-Seltzer.

It is pleasant and reassuring to believe in such "magic." We liked that kind of magic when we were children and we still respond favorably to quick and easy solutions as adults. If only we could find the right combination of ingredients, the right diet pill, the right weight control program, that headache, stomach-ache or eating problem we suffer from would be eliminated. We convince ourselves that our *only* responsibility is to experiment until we find the correct substance or diet. Like magic.

PROMOTING WEIGHT LOSS

Feeding our addictions is big business. So, too, is undoing the consequences of our destructive eating. Kate Parry, writing in the *Minneapolis Tribune*, explains, "Some people are living off the fat of the land and making a bundle. They are doing it by selling appetite suppressants, diet pills, weight-loss books, mechanical devices, and stints in health spas and fat farms."[6] We pay $10 billion a year for our temporary weight loss and our desire for quick and easy solutions for our eating problems.

As a consequence of contradictory values of our society, the dual emphasis on slenderness and food, "Weight control is a serious problem—32 percent of men and 40 percent of women ages 40 to 49 are at least 20 percent overweight."[7] Forty-five million Americans diet and lose weight

each year. Ninety-five percent gain it right back. Not included in these statistics are people who endlessly battle an extra 10 to 20 pounds or less.

THE THIN FIXATION

Ninety-five percent of the participants in weight control programs are women, and nearly half of these applicants appear to be of normal weight. More than 90 percent of anorexics, who diet themselves into starvation and emaciation, are female, as are almost all bulimics, who binge and then purge. Of female college students, 20 to 30 percent are bulimic.

Some of those popular before-and-after photos of "successful" dieters show curvaceous women who have reduced to a nearly emaciated state. When diet groups and clinics have bottom-line profit among their goals, how likely are they to discourage such damaging weight loss? Should they even try, their effectiveness would be limited, since women often have unrealistic images of their own bodies and carry weight loss to health-threatening extremes.

Men are victims of social programming too. Most of them have accepted the norm that slender women are most desirable. Female Foodaholics frequently report receiving negative comments about their weight or their bodies by significant males in their lives: a spouse, boyfriend, brother, father, or doctor. Almost universally, they place this male figure in an authority role and never question the validity of his judgments. The dynamics of these interactions can go to ludicrous extremes. Angie is a slender woman whose boyfriend, Vince, would pinch her minimally-fleshed abdomen as she sat beside him, chiding her for getting fat. Strange? What is stranger still, *she believed him* and tried to lose weight! Unfortunately, both men and women in our society seem determined to deny that women are blessed with hips, breasts, and stomachs.

Current standards for fitness and slender bodies are beginning to have a greater effect on men, especially young men, gay men, and men who have a strong desire to look younger. However, Kim Chernin, author of *The Obsession: Reflections on The Tyranny of Slenderness*, believes that men in general feel less uncomfortable being overweight in this society. She states that studies and statistics indicate that the response to men who are overweight is less acute and less damaging. This information has been gleaned from interviews and actual statistics about the relative success in job interviews of overweight males and females.[8]

Marcia Millman, author of *Such A Pretty Face*, and associate professor of Sociology at the University of California at Santa Cruz, has a similar thesis:

> Because physical appearance is so consequential for women, we attempt to change our looks in order to change our lives, while in our places, men would think about their work or achievements in the world. Although both pursuits can become ungratifying and alienating, the focus on physical appearance is more trivial, more unrealistic, more certain to maintain us as objects rather than subjects. . . . The point is that human potential and unhappiness are tragically wasted by our society's emphasis on physical beauty.[9]

Our cultural ideal of the attractive body as decidedly slender, or even downright skinny, has not only financial but psychological implications. Those judged overweight by current social norms punish themselves in an attempt to comply with those norms. "Too often a series of unsuccessful diet attempts and unattained weight loss goals become part of a vicious cycle, in which feelings of despair and self-condemnation lead to further overeating and additional weight gain."[10]

"Not only are the overweight the most stigmatized group in the United States, but fat people are expected to participate in their own degradation by agreeing with others who taunt them. If any other stigmatized group were similarly derided on television and radio or in the movies, lawsuits would result,"[11] claims Jack Kamerman of the Department of Sociology and Social Work at Kean College of New Jersey.

Unrealistic standards for slenderness have been reflected in the insurance charts, which are currently undergoing revision. People who are heavier are not less healthy. The recent Framingham study shows that men have to be more than 25 percent overweight to affect life expectancy and that weight and mortality have little correlation for women.[12]

While our society has an intense fixation on health, fitness, and diet, it is ironic that the majority of dieters focus not on improving their health with nutritious, well-balanced diets, but on losing weight with rigid, inadequate regimens. Some people cannot lose more weight because their bodies have adapted to excessive dieting. Their more efficient use of food is a built-in mechanism which protects them from their self-inflicted starvation.[13] So they have to radically curtail intake to lose weight, and then rapidly regain it when they resume normal eating. Obsessed with their weight, they feel guilty, deem themselves failures, and accept blame from physicians, diet counselors, and family members.

What a pity it is that 45 million people are experiencing all the physical and emotional hazards of seesawing through life on the diet-binge yo-yo. They keep themselves from being happy, living life, and feeling content with themselves because of this obsession. Many will go to their graves still fretting over that last five pounds.

NOTES

1. Robert T. Smith, *The Minneapolis Tribune*, March 22, 1982.
2. Robert T. Smith, *The Minneapolis Tribune*, June 29, 1981.
3. Paul A. Stitt, *Fighting The Food Giants*. (Manitowoc, WI: Natural Press, 1980), pp. 85–88.
4. From *Meganutrition* by Richard A. Kunin, M.D. Copyright 1980 by Richard A. Kunin, M.D. Used with permission of McGraw-Hill Book Company, p. 120.
5. Emily Fox Kales, "The 'Diet-Resistant' Personality," *Obesity and Metabolism Journal*, Vol. 1, No. 2, p. 123.
6. Kate Parry, "The Diet Industry: Some Gotta Lose, Some Gotta Win." *The Minneapolis Tribune*, October 8, 1981.
7. Gordon Slovut: Medicine. *The Minneapolis Star*, May 4, 1981.
8. Kim Chernin, "Donahue Transcript #12111," p. 19.
9. Marcia Millman, "When I'm Thin I'll Be Perfect," *Savvy*, February 1980, p. 36.
10. Kales, "Diet-Resistant Personality," p. 120.
11. Dava Sobel, "Science Times: Psychological Factors." *The New York Times*, February 24, 1981.
12. William Bennett and Joel Gurin, "Do Diets Really Work?" *Science*, March 1982.
13. *Ibid*.

8

Compliance
and Rebellion:
Anorexia and Bulimia

BULIMIA: ELLEN'S STORY

Ellen has an average-size body and is well-proportioned. She has an out-going personality and appears to be very healthy. She has always eaten normally when in the presence of other people. But, by herself, Ellen had a habit of consuming enormous quantities of food and subsequently forc-ing herself to vomit. When she finally entered therapy at the age of 24, she had been binge-eating and vomiting for six years.

Ellen developed this bulimic behavior—dieting, then binge-eating and purging—after her father's admonition that she should lose weight, fol-lowed by the move of her best friend to another state. She was equally obsessed with being thin *and* with eating. Her intense fear of fat and food-deprivation combined to create intense conflict and a painful cycle of binge-eating, then vomiting or the use of laxatives to rid herself of the unwanted calories and discomfort. A typical binge for Ellen consisted of 5,000 to 50,000 calories, mostly sweets and carbohydrates.

Ellen would induce vomiting several times daily. She would eat a "bad food" and then follow it with great quantities of other food. "I can always get rid of it," she reasoned. Ellen's binges consumed an inordinate amount of her time, energy, and money, leaving few resources for social life or other ordinary pursuits.

After graduating from college and entering into the working world, Ellen mostly confined her binges to weekends. She kept tempting foods out of the house, and adhered to a rigid diet during the week. But on weekends, when she ate at a restaurant or someone's home, she would convince herself that she had lost control when she ate either slightly too much or food not on her diet. On her way home, she would throw up her hands in shame and despair and decide to "go all the way." She would shop for a large supply of junk food. Upon consuming this enormous amount of food, she would purge herself of it.

Ellen's binges were often planned, secret happenings. She usually binged at the same time of the day or week. Although the original "bad food" was one she desired and enjoyed, once Ellen turned her conviction that she was out of control into a self-fulfilling prophecy, she no longer experienced any pleasure in her rapid, compulsive eating.

Ellen would also binge when she experienced an emotion she felt powerless to handle. She thought: "I'm angry and I shouldn't feel angry." Or she felt the physical uneasiness of an unpleasant emotion which she did not identify. At these times, Ellen was prone to stuff her emotions down her throat with lots of food and symbolically vomit them up again, rejected, and "handled." In this way, she achieved a temporary, but false sense of relief. Sometimes she even felt "high." Then she would shame herself for what she had done and begin the binge- and- vomit cycle again. It had become an addiction for Ellen, a tried and true method of handling her feelings.

Bulimia, Ellen's type of Foodaholism, is rarely life-threatening. It does, however, cause adverse effects such as sore throat, swelling/inflammation of salivary glands, and damaged knuckles. Excessive cavities and erosion of tooth enamel, muscle weakness, lethargy, and menstrual irregularities may also occur. Electrolyte disturbances result in chemical imbalance affecting metabolism and emotional stability.

Ellen sees herself in Dr. Hilde Bruch's words: "People suffering from eating disorders experience themselves as *acting only in response* to demands coming from others, and not doing anything *because they want to*."[1] (Emphasis added.)

Ellen's View of her Healthy Rebellion

"It is unfortunate that we choose to shorten our lives, endanger our health, isolate ourselves, diminish our energy, and feed our self-hate as a means to rebel against others' expectations of us. I worked so hard at being nice that I rarely admitted that I was angry, even to myself. I was angry at being watched and judged by people who imposed their standards on me. I was angry at people who acted as if they knew best what I should be eating. I was angry at being told how I should look and feel. I was angry at being judged strictly on the basis of my appearance. I was angry about being constantly misunderstood, criticized and discounted.

"I needed to develop a new attitude. I had to acknowledge my right to protect myself, take care of myself and communicate directly in my own behalf. I needed to learn to say a whole bunch of 'no's' instead of saying 'no' with the food I ate or the size I had become.

"As I allowed myself to experience my rebellious feelings and use my 'no's' instead of abusing my body, I began to experience my anger. I felt more and more angry. I decided that I was a very angry person. I felt frightened by all these negative feelings, and I also got feedback from others about my being selfish, inconsiderate, touchy, grouchy, feisty, crotchety, and impossible to live with.

"In spite of all this, I think it's significant that I'm not just 'nice' anymore.

"For people like me who have always bent over backwards to be nice, to be good to others, to be kind and thoughtful, considerate and pleasing, it was difficult to accept my new, angry stage. Yes, it was a stage. I consider it a developmental stage that I skipped earlier in life. In the process of becoming a compliant, adaptive, nice person, I passed over my limit-setting, rebellious phase a number of times. I needed to stop scaring myself about the probable dire consequences of saying 'no' and to experience how a calm, firm refusal rarely has long-term, disastrous consequences. Now that I am skilled at taking care of myself and being assertive, I no longer need to be so angry. When I ask for what I want or refuse what I don't want, I don't feel angry."

KATHLEEN'S STORY—A CELEBRATION![2]

"I have been inspired by Mary's celebrating her recovery and her graduation from the Foodaholics' group to acknowledge mine, not from group but from bulimia, a secret, an anger, a power over my body.

"I haven't spoken much about bulimia. I didn't know the *word* a year ago. Now I have realized the extent of my recovery. Twelve years ago my friend Jim said he could vomit at will. I was amazed, oddly impressed. What control! What novelty! (We were seekers of vision, my friends and I, innovators, outlaws.) The Romans did it, in a lust for pleasure. Ate and vomited, vomited and ate. 'It's just the reverse of swallowing,' Jim said. And it was; it was easy.

"At seventeen I already had a woman's body, soft and round. Thighs that touched when I walked and stood. A stomach that curved. A body that I hated. But then . . . I could feast with my friends and not gain weight. It was a comfort, a convenience, a power. When I lost grasp of my other powers, it would still be there. The comfort of a full belly. The ability to avoid its consequences, the right to remain a *girl*.

"It has been six months since I have made myself vomit. Six months after ten years of binging and purging—once, five times, eight times a day. Eating and throwing up dozens of donuts, a whole loaf of toast, batch after batch of pancakes. Flour on the floor, batter in my hair, a hole burnt in my jacket from leaning over the stove. Too desperate to cook and eat to take my jacket off.

"After six months I recognize hunger. I eat and it feels good. It feels solid. I feel the nutritive power, the energy, move through my body. I feed myself. I no longer want to puke my heart out. I rest my hand on my belly, a woman's belly, and my body feels whole. I finally feel whole."

ANOREXIA: GEORGIA'S STORY

At age 16, Georgia had a nearly fatal episode of an extreme form of Food-aholism called anorexia nervosa. Although anorexia means lack of hunger, Georgia had starved herself to a state of emaciation, not because she was not hungry, but because she desired to look extremely thin. In spite of the fact that she was ravenously hungry and constantly thought about food, she forced herself to eat so little that her weight continued to drop. She talked about food, shopped for her family, and prepared gourmet meals of which she ate little.

Georgia ran 10 miles daily after forcing herself through a highly rigorous program of warm-up calisthenics. As she exercised, she felt she was controlling or mastering her body and her life. When she failed to follow her routine perfectly, she was convinced she had lost control. Her regimen seemed to be a form of self-punishment. In fact, when she ate too much or was too sorely tempted to eat, she would force herself to run again or to run further.

Georgia's parents, Zoe and Bill, were distressed about their daughter's physical condition. They were also disturbed by their own helplessness in changing her behavior. Georgia had been a model child, a considerate, adaptive, soft-spoken youngster who rarely misbehaved. When she turned 15, she and they began to quarrel about her failure to eat and Georgia's role in the family system became that of identified patient or scapegoat, the object of negative focus. They were all certain that if only Georgia would shape up, they could be a happy family again.

No matter what Zoe and Bill said or did, Georgia would only eat minute quantities of food. She moved the food around on her plate, found fault with it, fed it to the dog, wrapped it in her napkin, and otherwise found ways to eat sparingly.

Georgia continued to lose weight. She remained oblivious to the reality of her skin and bones image in the mirror. She was indifferent to the opinions of others when they expressed concern about her extreme thinness.

Although Georgia acted with determination and self-assurance, she was suffering greatly. She experienced a variety of both physical and emotional symptoms. She usually felt cold. She had an embarrassing growth of furry body hair. She had ceased to menstruate, and sometimes she experienced lightheadedness or fatigue caused by her low blood pressure. The scale seemed to determine whether she would have a good or a bad day. Thinking about food and her time spent exercising left her little time or interest in her peers.

Even though the whole family responded to her eating behavior and it appeared that she had the power to control them, she actually felt misunderstood, and powerless to affect anyone or anything except her own body.

Georgia actually felt superior when she heard people discussing their weight problems. Her self-esteem and her weight were desperately bound together, since it was the only area in which she felt superior. Her body seemed to be the only thing in life over which she had any control, and control it she must.

Georgia's weight loss and eating patterns served positive purposes for her and her family. Georgia finally got some of the attention she craved. As a good little girl, she had been mostly ignored.

By serving as the focus of Zoe and Bill's attention, Georgia invited them to deal with her rather than with their marital relationship, which was ailing. She admits now she feared they would separate. Zoe and Bill were grateful for their shared interest in Georgia's eating problem and the opportunity to avoid facing their disappointment and anger about the lack of communication, closeness, and joy in their relationship.

Zoe and Bill's handling of Georgia's failure to eat reflected how they really felt about each other. It was the only subject about which they freely disagreed. Bill would scold Georgia and issue ultimatums. Zoe blamed Bill for being too dictatorial and domineering. Bill accused Zoe of catering to Georgia, yet not taking adequate care of her as her condition rapidly deteriorated. When one parent would talk to Georgia about eating more, the other parent would argue or sidetrack the communication. Quarreling resulted, enabling Georgia to once again escape without eating.

No one really understood the terror Georgia was living with. When the scale indicated a weight gain she would panic. If she compliantly ate more to please her mother, father, or doctor, she perceived her slightly distended stomach as grotesque and felt physically uncomfortable.

Ultimately, Georgia was hospitalized for three months. She received both the medical and psychological treatment she needed. She was not released until her weight reached a certain level. After her release, Georgia continued to maintain the weight she and her hospital psychotherapist had established. She was still terribly thin, but not starving herself.

In her early twenties, Georgia voluntarily sought therapy again. She feared her growing compulsion to lose weight and engage in a rigidly structured and punishing exercise regimen. Like 25 to 50 percent of all anorexics, Georgia experienced a recurrence of symptoms.[3] Fortunately, she was not among the 38 percent who are rehospitalized[4] or the 15 to 21 percent for whom anorexia proves to be fatal.[5]

Georgia *appears* to have an eating disorder different from the one Ellen and Kathleen have; that is not true. Studies show that 25 percent[6] to 50 percent of anorexics exhibit binge-purge behavior or are actively bulimic.[7] A significant number of anorexics become bulimic after they have attained normal weight.[8] Another study shows that 50 percent of bulimics have a history of anorexia.[9] Since the disorders of anorexia and bulimia overlap to such an extent, it is not surprising that people who suffer from them often have similar thinking patterns, personality traits, and feelings.

SIMILARITIES IN ANOREXIA
AND BULIMIA

Studies indicate that the following characteristics are common to both anorexics and bulimics. It should be pointed out, however, that these similarities are generalized to anorexics and bulimics as *groups* and that marked individual variations do exist.

1. Body/Identity
- 90 to 95 percent of both anorexics and bulimics are female.
- Both are at war with their own bodies and caught in a love/hate, survive/die conflictual relationship with themselves.
- Both share an inability or deficiency in recognizing hunger and other bodily sensations.
- Both have a basic disturbance in self-awareness/identity.
- Both have distorted body images. They perceive themselves as fatter or larger than others perceive them.

2. Control
- Both have issues of control and feel powerless within their families. They feel unseen and perceive little response to their needs.
- Both are obsessed with food, the amount eaten or not eaten, how eaten, and when eaten. Thus, both are fearful of food, since they have given it great meaning and control over themselves.
- Both are grandiose in that they believe they are in control: the anorexic, finally, of her body and life; and the bulimic, of her body and emotions.

3. Personality
- Both tend to be intelligent, achievement oriented, and perfectionistic.
- Both were well-behaved as children, often shy, timid, "good little girls."
- Both feel intense isolation and lack close relationships.
- Both experience a pervasive sense of shame. They experience being irreparably and unspeakably defective.[10] An intense fear of exposure accompanies their shame. The anorexic defends herself with rebellion and a superior air. The bulimic covers her shame by using her intelligence, poise, and smooth words.

4. Beliefs

- Both believe the cultural myth that being thin will solve their problems.
- Both see themselves, others, situations, and the world in terms of black-and-white. There is only right or wrong, good or bad, perfection or failure. "If I can't be perfect, I must be worthless. If I am not somebody, I am nobody. If I'm not in complete control, I lose all control."

DIFFERENCES BETWEEN ANOREXICS AND BULIMICS

- The anorexic experiences great power as her illness develops. The family focuses its attention and concern on her and joins her in becoming obsessed with her weight. The bulimic conceals her disorder from the family. Whatever they may observe or hear, they generally ignore.
- The anorexic is generally shy and withdrawn, less articulate and more reserved and withdrawn (except when she is stubbornly refusing food). The bulimic is often outgoing and highly verbal.
- The anorexic often feels superior because of the way she believes she controls her body and her environment. The bulimic feels ashamed and a failure in her binges and purges.
- For the anorexic, her eating disorder is a way of gaining control personally. For the bulimic it may be a way of letting go of control, not being perfect or responsible all of the time.
- The anorexic is often asexual. She wishes to deny her female body and her sexuality, and might even yearn to be a child again. The bulimic usually has more sexual experience. With the onset of the eating disorder, however, she may express less interest in being sexual.
- Families of anorexics tend to be smaller in number and are likely to have more daughters than sons. Families of bulimics tend to be larger.
- The bulimic may also be alcoholic. She may have problems with other compulsive behaviors and impulse control such as shoplifting, suicide, and self-mutilation.
- The bulimic's mother often has a problem with abusive eating too.
- The anorexic more often comes from an upper middle class family, though anorexia is fast losing its class[11] and age[12] bias.
- Bulimics are generally older than anorexics and span a broader age range, 11 to 45 years in one study.[13] Anorexia most often occurs in pre-pubertal children or adolescents.

FAMILY SYSTEMS

Anorexic/bulimic families tend to exaggerate the patterns which are prevalent in Foodaholic families. Boundaries are ambiguous and it is often unclear to whom an emotion, problem, responsibility, or physical sensation belongs. Family members are intrusive and tend to mind each other's business. They avoid experiencing and talking about conflict or negative emotions, presenting a "united front" to the world that is actually a closed family system. The family exerts intense pressure on individuals to conform to rigid family rules involving behavior and appearance. Deviations or differences are poorly tolerated. A Minneapolis therapist identifies parents of children with eating disorders as frequently lacking empathy with the children's feelings and needs.[14]

Salvador Minuchin, one of the nations foremost family therapists in the treatment of anorexia nervosa, graphically characterizes the anorexic family system. Typically, these families are child-oriented, highly enmeshed, quick to deny that family conflict exists and one or both parents maintain a particularly strong connection to their family of origin.[15]

In spite of proclaiming family intimacy and congeniality, these families actually share little genuine affection and emotion. Distancing tactics may be especially marked between the parents, who often smother their children with interfering attention as a substitute for elements lacking in this relationship. They often undermine each other's efforts to communicate with and discipline offspring. This dynamic results in failure to get the anorexic child to eat.

Children in these families are socialized to meet family expectations, represent the family well, and to maintain a high degree of loyalty to family values. The family is regarded as a life focus, and the children often do not develop the necessary skills to effectively interact with peers at school and work. There is an emphasis within the family on bodily functions and somatic complaints; family control is maintained under a veil of concern.[16]

Although much less research has been published on bulimic family systems, some patterns are emerging. Among them are histories of severe depression and food or alcohol abuse.

TREATMENT

If you suspect you are anorexic or bulimic, I hope you will take good care of yourself by seeking professional evaluation or help. It may be easier for you to do so if you know more about what to expect.

You may have a nutritionally induced thinking disorder and emotional disturbance if you have been anorexic for a while, or have rapidly lost 20 percent or more of your body weight. Medical treatment and perhaps hospitalization may be necessary before psychotherapy can have a noticeable effect. Nutrition therapy and weight gain are required to cure symptoms of starvation. Professional support is vital in learning to cope with feelings and the details of a new eating program. Reorganizing of thinking, emotional issues and life itself can begin in earnest when you are functioning better physically.

There are many therapists using a wide variety of methods to treat anorexia and bulimia, ranging from psychoanalysis to behavior modification, from family therapy to self-help groups. Seeking professional help is largely a matter of finding a therapist whose approach and personality are consistent with your needs. Academic degrees are perhaps less important to effectiveness than is experience in the successful treatment of eating disorders. If you are also abusing alcohol or drugs, it is most important to first consult a counselor or center specializing in diagnosis and treatment of chemical dependency.

You need not like or agree with everything a therapist says or does. A more important criterion is that the therapist supports you in being a whole person—disagreeing or voicing your opinions, dealing with your anger—and that you are encouraged to participate in designing your recovery program. Seek a therapist who will help you assert yourself and develop your own value system. It is in your best interest to select a therapist who believes in your recovery and will strengthen your sense of hope. Recovery represents a progressive improvement of emotional and physical health, as well as a lessening of the food obsession.

Don't hesitate to seek another therapist if, after a reasonable period of time, you feel dissatisfied with your progress or the approach. Second opinions are encouraged. The National Association of Anorexia and Associated Disorders (ANAD) offers information and support, as well as a referral list of therapists throughout the United States.[17]

WHAT MATTERS
OR MAKES A DIFFERENCE IN THERAPY

To offer a more concrete idea of what you may need and expect from therapy, former anorexics and bulimics have cited the following as important to their recovery

Self-Acceptance

- Acceptance of my body.
- My self-esteem has improved. I may act rotten at times, but I know now I am not a rotten human being.
- Acceptance of my vomiting behavior helped me let go of it.
- I felt less shame when I learned that others share similar experiences and behaviors.
- I no longer want to disappear. I know now I want to have an impact and deserve to be responded to by others.
- I have learned to accept my limitations and to be flexible. I may do some backsliding. I don't have to be perfect, even in getting well.
- Not having to "perform" in order to win approval from the therapist allowed me to trust people more.

Self-Care

- I learned to take better care of myself.
- I began by nurturing a teddy bear stand-in for myself, and moved on to letting others nurture me. It helped me to finally recognize and care for the sad little girl in me.
- I learned that I am not powerless and that I can get my needs met.
- I learned to say "no."
- Learning how to deal with anger rather than puking it off on the world helped me a lot.

Modeling

- Positive interaction was modeled by male/female co-leaders.
- Facilitators acted like "healthy parents."
- Seeing others improve gave me hope.
- The group responded to my needs like a healthy, caring family.

Both therapist and client must believe there is hope for recovery from the eating disorder. Bev, the Minneapolis therapist referred to earlier in this chapter relates the story of a young woman named Jeanine who came for help in recovering from bulimia. Jeanine expressed great doubt about getting better because she had been reading about poor prognosis in the treatment of what she recognized as her disorder—bulimia.

Bev replied, "Well, I don't know too much about bulimia myself, but I'm sure you will get better."[18] This leap of faith on the therapist's part may literally have saved Jeanine's life. In therapy several months later Jeanine confided in Bev that she had decided to kill herself if she were offered no immediate help or hope of recovery.

Anorexia and bulimia are complicated and painful eating disorders. Strides are being made in treatment and recovery which can end the painful silence and break down the walls of isolation typically experienced by those suffering from these disorders. You may be on the road to recovery when you understand, as 19-year-old Martha did, that "it doesn't have anything to do with food!" She was ecstatic over her new awareness, that her recovery was related to issues of family/trust/nurturance/control/lack of control/identity. Martha obtained the help she needed and worked through these issues and so can you!

NOTES

1. Hilde Bruch, M.D., *Eating Disorders, Obesity, Anorexia Nervosa and The Person Within*. (New York: Basic Books, 1973), p. 216.
2. Reprinted with permission of Kathleen A. Rudy, Minneapolis, MN 1983.
3. H. Moldofsky and P.E. Garfinkel, "Problems of Treatment of Anorexia Nervosa." *Canadian Psychiatric Association Journal*, 1974, *19*, pp. 169–175.
4. P.J. Dally, *Anorexia Nervosa*. (New York: Grune and Stratton, 1969), p. 120.
5. Diagnostic and Statistical Manual of Mental Disorders (3rd Edition, 1980). (Washington, DC: American Psychiatric Association.)
6. Hilde Bruch, M.D., "Developmental Considerations of Anorexia Nervosa and Obesity." *Canadian Journal of Psychiatry*, June 1981, *26* (4), p. 213.
7. Casper, R.C. et al, "The Incidence and Clinical Significance of Bulimia in Patients with Anorexia Nervosa." *Archives of General Psychiatry*, 1980, *37*, pp. 1030–1035.
   L.K.G. Hsu, A.H. Crisp and B. Harding, "Outcome of Anorexia Nervosa. *Lancet*, 1979, i. pp. 61–65.
   R.L. Pyle, J.E. Mitchell, and E.D. Eckert, "Bulimia." *Journal of Clinical Psychiatry*, 1981.
8. G. Russell, "Bulimia Nervosa: An Animous Variant of Anorexia Nervosa. *Psychological Medicine*, 1979, *9*, pp. 429–446.
9. Jane Wardle and Helen Reinart. "Binge Eating, A Theoretical Review." *British Journal of Clinical Psychology*, June 1981, *20* (2), p. 97.
10. Gershen Kaufman, "The Meaning of Shame: Toward a Self-Affirming Identity." *Journal of Counseling Psychology*, 1974, *21* (6), pp. 568–574.
11. Salvador Minuchin, Bernice L. Rosman, and Lester Baker, *Psychoso-*

matic Families. (Cambridge, MA: Harvard University Press, 1978), pp. 59–62.

12. Interview with Beverly Welsh, M.S.W., Family and Children's Service, Minneapolis, Minnesota, June 30, 1982.

13. Richard L. Pyle, James E. Mitchell, and Elke D. Eckert, "Bulimia: A Report of 34 Cases." *Journal of Clinical Psychiatry*, February 1981, *42* (2), p. 61.

14. Welsh interview.

15. Minuchin, *Psychosomatic Families*, pp. 59–62.

16. *Ibid.*

17. National Association of Anorexia and Associated Disorders, Box 271, Highland Park, IL 60035. (312) 831–3438.

18. Welsh interview.

9

How Our Destructive Eating or Size Speaks for Us

The body size and eating patterns we Foodaholics cultivate have a variety of meanings for us and for others. The conscious and unconscious choices we make regarding what we will look like and how we will eat can serve many purposes beyond the obvious ones. The concept of choosing our size does not apply to unchangeable biological characteristics such as inherited body configuration, height, frame size, and setpoint,[1] which is the specific weight toward which we naturally gravitate, despite episodes of gaining or losing.

At an earlier age, at some level of consciousness, each of us chose a certain mode of eating behavior or type of appearance. At that time, our choice of behavior met our need or served our purpose. Instead of feeling victimized by our body size, guilty, helpless, or inadequate to effect change, we can feel more powerful when we begin to notice and accept the purposefulness of our behavior and to congratulate ourselves for discovering such ingenious methods of surviving or getting what we wanted.

We Foodaholics can feel more in charge of our lives and our eating if we take responsibility for our choices—our decisions to behave in a certain way. In changing from a passive role or an angry one to a responsible one, evaluating these decisions will be an integral part of our recovery. Originally, our choice may have served our purpose well. Is it still a choice that represents our best interests? If so, we have validated our decision. If not, then we are capable of redeciding—changing our mind and, ultimately, our behavior.

Bob's outlook has been passive and helpless. It seems that life just "happens" to him. He doubts that he has made choices: "What could I have done? Our house was always loaded with luscious baked goods, and Mom kept pushing me to eat. My wife wants me to diet, but she won't stop baking for our teenage sons." And: "It's impossible for me to eat moderately. I work with food all day." Bob honestly thought there weren't alternatives until he began to explore further: "Do my siblings choose to eat abusively also? Did they choose to join Mom's Clean Plate Club? How did others handle Mom's food-pushing? What did I gain, however subtly, from Mom when I agreed to eat her food offerings? Do my co-workers munch all day long at work too? The ones who don't, how do they approach food differently? How do they view themselves differently?" When we Foodaholics think we have a choice, we can ask ourselves questions as Bob is doing. We can observe, imitate, and adopt the healthier patterns we observe in others.

If our destructive eating is a socially condoned abuse to which we have, out of ignorance, subjected ourselves, we can seek the information and support we need to make healthy changes. When our destructive pattern is a metaphor or symbol for our other unresolved problems, it will be difficult to switch to a healthy eating program without first recognizing and resolving the underlying problem.

The following is an overview of some common life purposes or motivations served by developing and maintaining abusive eating behavior, food obsession, or obesity.

AVOIDANCE

Being obsessed with food or appearance can help us avoid acknowledging or handling some painful or scary aspects of our lives. I invite you to do an experiment that can help you understand yourself. You need not share it with anyone else. I will give you a sentence to complete in ten different ways. Say aloud whatever pops into your head, and tape, write, or dictate your words. Work very quickly.

If I weren't thinking about eating/dieting, I would . . ."

_____

(Repeat nine more times.)
_____

_____

_____

_____

_____

_____

_____

While doing the preceding exercise, Tess said:

- I would wonder why Bob [her fiance] changed the subject when I
  was talking about our relationship last night.
- I would miss the friends with whom I've lost contact.
- I would feel hurt that he cancelled our dinner date Sunday.

Tess slowed down, got wide-eyed, then tearful. "You know, when I stop
and think," she said, "I'm really unhappy about the way Bob is treating
me." Then she enumerated the many ways which he communicated to
her through words and actions that he didn't value her as a person. In spite
of his treating her as if she is unimportant, Bob was very possessive,
demanding that Tess be constantly available in case he decided to be
with her. By seeking to appease Bob's anger and meet his possessive
demands, Tess had allowed her relationships with friends and coworkers
to deteriorate.

Tess continued: "I've put all my eggs in one basket. It's a pretty
one—let's say 'lined in satin'—because he's successful, handsome, and
charming in public. I am flattered that he wants to marry me, but my
satin-lined basket is beginning to feel cold, lonely, and uncomfortable.
I'm afraid he's far more important to me than I am to him."

Tess decided to reestablish contact with her friends. She rejoined the bowling league and scheduled time with her buddies even though Bob might be available at those times. Several months later Tess broke her engagement after struggling to cope with Bob's negative reaction to her reduced willingness to plan her whole life around him. Her less predictable singleness had become more comfortable and attractive than a secure but stifling future with Bob.

After six or seven "If I weren't" statements to his small group in the Foodaholics' class, Tom confessed: "If I weren't thinking about food all the time, I would be bored out of my gourd at work!" He enumerated all the things he hated about his job, how much he wanted to switch careers, but how trapped he felt. Others in the group shared similar predicaments and supplied leads for career counseling, information gathering, and employment opportunities.

Thereafter, when Tom caught himself thinking about food, he checked whether he was avoiding strong feelings about his job. Nearly a year later he found an exciting position with greater potential for growth.

Another way we use the avoidance technique is when we duck responsibility by blaming our fat or abusive eating:

- That's why I didn't get the position/promotion.
- That's why I don't date or have a poor social life.
- That's why my spouse and I don't get along.
- That's why my family is always criticizing me.
- That's why my supervisor/friends/neighbors treat me poorly.
- That's why my co-workers ignore or exclude me.
- That's why I don't change careers/start a career/go to school.
- That's why I don't have much fun or enjoy life.
- That's why I don't like myself.

If we blame our problems on our overweight or overeating, then weighing or eating less will probably be a traumatic experience for us. We may be expecting to become suddenly successful in our social, academic, family, or career lives. Failure to achieve this dramatic transformation will be a rude shock to us blamers! What will we have to blame when we have changed our size and eating behavior but, in all other respects, we are still the same?

We can use obesity as an avoidance technique in order to deny some of the basic facts of life. We may be choosing to ignore the critical, judgmental side of ourselves or others. Then, too, other character defects might come into focus when we are no longer fat. We may be using our size as a self-fulfilling prophecy if we assume that being overweight is a handicapping condition.

Believing we will be different people when we are thin is like believing we will be different people when we move to Arizona. We forget that no matter where we go or how we change physically, we take along our self-defeating behavior, our established patterns of mishandling interpersonal relationships and our critical inner dialogue.

What We Are Hiding From

- We may not want to see how our constant complaining and negative mind-set alienates people.
- We could be hiding from the fact that our demanding way or clinging dependence scares people away.
- Perhaps we don't really want to know that our competitiveness, poor listening skills, or uncanny ability to keep the spotlight on ourselves makes it unrewarding for others to converse with us.
- We won't bear the pain of acknowledging how inadequate we feel. Instead we keep promising ourselves that our mumbling responses and downcast glance will go away when we are thin.
- We won't face the fact that others will believe we are important when we think so ourselves.

ADAPTATION

We are behaving adaptively when we agree to play a certain role or behave in a given way in response to the expectations or behaviors of others. Usually, a group of us who live or work together will form a "family system"—a constellation of roles and behaviors that may feel familiar to us. Our sense of familiarity probably indicates that we played similar roles in our families of origin.

Pleasing or Placating

Overweight or abusive eating can be a means of conforming, a way of meeting our families' or society's expectations of us.

Perhaps we decided to eat heartily as children in order to please our parents. We may have eaten because of our fear that otherwise they wouldn't like us or take care of us. Or maybe we have traditionally received lots of attention for being "good eaters" or cleaning our plates.

Scapegoat

A scapegoat can attract negative attention for eating behavior or size. As children, we may have believed that such behavior could draw attention away from marital discord or other family troubles, could ease tension in the family, or could keep some family secrets: deviant sexual behaviors, relationship problems, craziness, chemical dependency, mistakes, failures, hate, or physical abuse.

Body Image

Our adaptations may center around maintaining a certain body size or body image. Until our feelings, ideas, and decisions about body images are exposed and dealt with, they will continue to influence how we look and what we choose to eat.

We who were exposed to actual or threatened food deprivation may feel more secure when we are protected by an overabundance of food and flesh. Having grown up hungry during the Depression, Arthur discovered that his padding and paunch were for him symbols of success and prosperity. When he became thin, he again experienced the anxiety of his impoverished youth. Arthur prefers to remain thin and deal with his anxiety through therapy rather than to cope with his high blood pressure and the necessary medication.

Andrea is a very maternal woman who believes that an ample, well-fleshed appearance more adequately reflects who she is and represents her to society as a good mother. She learned in childhood that slim women are "slinky, sexy, and not very interested in nurturing children." Andrea chooses to continue to maintain her full-bodied appearance but has ceased eating abusively.

Loyalty

A decision to be loyal could also be getting in the way of our recovery. We may have an underlying belief that we must not outdo a parent, sibling, spouse, or friend. Maybe we're not supposed to be thinner, happier, or less abusive in our eating than the significant person. Perhaps we have dared to surpass this person in our career success or the quality of our relationships. Then our fat or destructive eating could be a statement to that other: "See, I can't manage my body/eating, so you can still feel superior." We have, in essence, agreed to be responsible for another person's feelings.

We may behave as if we believed the myth that the elements of happiness, success, and self-esteem come in measurable and limited quantities. We may believe that if we maintain the optimum balance and proper share of these elements in our relationships, and carefully guard against taking too much for ourselves, that everything in our lives will be just fine.

In some families or systems, suffering is the currency with which people bargain. Martyrdom is the desired state and the person who best achieves it wins the competition! People act as if they believe that time, money, food, comfort, new clothes, fun, joy, and friends are in short supply. We may hear or believe:

- Life is tough. Don't enjoy it. (We feel guilty in order to make up for having too much of any of the short-supply items.)
- We all have our cross to bear. (Ours is a food problem.)
- Pride goeth before a fall. (We dare not like or accept ourselves.)
- Others have worse problems. (We aren't entitled to complain or to want more from life.)
- Count your blessings. (My spouse/friend/boss used to treat me well, so I'll ignore the abuse or put-downs I receive from that person.)
- Happiness has to be earned. (I have to work hard, but I will never become perfect enough to deserve it.)

It takes courage to subject our families or friends to the threat of our healthy eating and bodies, improved emotional state, and increased self-esteem. A recovering Foodaholic may be just as threatening to them as the newly-sober alcoholic is to his drinking buddies and family members whose lives revolve around alcohol. Consider the following:

- The sensitive, nurturing mother who feels a strong sense of failure and resentment when her 21-year-old daughter finally conquers long-standing weight and food abuse problems—*after* she moves from the family home . . .
- The well-meaning grandmother who thinks it's terribly "unkind" that her children no longer offer sugary treats to her five-year-old grandson—and lovingly keeps a secret supply for him . . .

- The food-buddy friendship between two middle age women that breaks down when one of them takes decisive new responsibility for her food intake and eating habits and no longer wishes to discuss food, diets, or trendy weight loss schemes . . .
- The young husband who feels cheated and unloved and the marriage that nearly falters when the wife acknowledges her sugar addiction and then completely eliminates this substance from family treats and meals . . .
- The close and caring older brother who is both a physician and a sugar addict questions his sister's reasons for abstaining from eating sweets, and then scolds her for her reply: "It's people like you, spreading old wives' tales, who make life difficult for people like me" . . .

In order to continue our recovery in the face of invitations to resume old behaviors and roles, we need to believe that we are responsible for only our own feelings and to seek the support of other recovering destructive eaters in order to withstand the pressure to remain practicing members of the Foodaholic system.

Rebellion

A negative form of adaptation is rebellion. It consists of actively or passively disobeying the norms or expectations of the system of which one is a member. A decision to rebel is not always made at the conscious level. Deciding to be fat/thin, or to eat a lot/little can be a way of saying: "You can't control me. I will show you. I will do the exact opposite of what you want." A member of any system can demand a lot of attention by violating the norms.

If others believe that "You can never be too thin," and "Food is to be eaten sparingly," we can proclaim our separate identities and create quite a stir by eating a lot. Some dedicated feminists *want* their larger bodies to proclaim their rebellion against an appearance-obsessed society.

Becoming slender can serve as a form of rebellion in those families or segments of society where slenderness is deemed unhealthy or where the loaded table and heaping plate are a way of life.

A bulimic who devours costly quantities of food and then purges it may be symbolically saying: "This is how much I think of all your food/money. So far as I'm concerned, it deserves to be stuffed right down the toilet."

Rebellion is one way of declaring our separateness and individuality.

It is healthy and appropriate behavior for those of us who bypassed natural rebellious stages earlier in our lives and have not yet completed this important developmental task. For those of us to whom rebellion is an old, established pattern in our lives, we might wish to evaluate whether or not it continues to meet our current needs.

Moving from adaptive behavior, which aims to please or displease others, to non-adaptive behavior keyed to pleasing ourselves, is an indication of our autonomy. Instead of operating simply as reactors or responders, we can increase our autonomy and become initiators by clearly establishing our own values. It *does* take time, thought, and effort to develop and then act upon our own values and needs.

In order to change from adaptive behavior focused on pleasing others to behavior that is pleasing to us, we will need some or all of the following: strong, caring people for ongoing support; practice of less threatening refusals while we gradually come to terms with the fact that people do *not* reject us for saying no; awareness and appreciation of the important ways in which we are self-sustaining; realization that we are no longer dependent upon others for care or approval; exploration of other methods for obtaining the recognition and positive reinforcement we need; professional help to support us as we work through unresolved issues from other times in our lives.

PROTECTION

Being fat can actually represent a way of taking care of ourselves. We could be protecting ourselves from too much attention, sexual overtures, closeness, or whatever it is we fear.

From Sexual Responses

Some rape or incest victims choose to become fat. They think that the fat will make them unattractive enough to be less vulnerable. This is magical thinking since sexual abuse victims range widely in attractiveness and girth. Rape and incest are more an expression of power and aggression than of sexuality. Might former victims who become obese be using their body size to claim more space and more power? Weight lifting has helped Margaret feel strong. She now says, "I know I can protect myself in the world." Learning self-defense techniques is an alternative to using fat as protection. It helps people know they are no longer fragile.

We may use our large size to help us avoid the wisecracks, innuendos, and propositions we experienced in a slender body.

RENEE'S STORY

Renee was a nightclub dancer years ago. She put on weight in her transition from showgirl to successful entrepreneur. Then, as she recovered from her destructive eating, she also lost her protective coating of flesh and discovered that she was attracting unwanted attention from men. Memories and emotions that this kind of attention evoked for Renee were distinctly unpleasant. She was not proud of her former career and now saw herself as a completely different woman. Renee's primary goals in the Foodaholics' therapy group were to strengthen her limit-setting methods and her self-image. She decided not to allow others to define her, to believe in her right to say "no" and practice it. She learned how to be assertive and discourage comments about her body. Instead she focused attention on her intelligence and professional accomplishments as a businesswoman.

Whether or not we have a sexual partner, we can use abusive eating to sedate our sexual feelings. We can use our size to place both physical and psychological distance between ourselves and a potential or established relationship. We may believe that as we grow larger we are less sexually attractive, but many obese people would strongly disagree with this idea. Body size, in and of itself, is not the primary factor that determines sexual attractiveness. The kinds of signals we send out when we do *not* want to become involved are much more important and affecting than body weight.

Distancing with our body size can be a way of avoiding temptation—we don't trust ourselves and our sexual feelings. Or, we could be protecting our partner, who may be threatened by our possibly attracting a new partner.

From Attention

We may use large body size as an excuse to hide in dark corners and dark clothes so that few people will pay attention to us. Being in the spotlight may be frightening. Perhaps we don't think we deserve attention or positive strokes.

From Success

We might hide behind our fat and continue our destructive eating behavior in order to protect ourselves from a fear of personal success. If we were of normal size and properly nourished to have boundless energy, we might be expected to accomplish much more. We are afraid we would have to actually begin to recognize and work with our potential or, worse yet, face the possibility of our failure.

From Closeness

The physical distance fat puts between us and other people is desirable when we want to keep emotional distance between ourselves and others. Perhaps we have experienced a devouring or domineering person in our lives and assume all relationships are like that. Or perhaps we were reared in an environment where people did not know how to be open and close to each other, and so we feel inadequate and afraid to relate in that manner. Maybe we "know" that if we let people get close enough to know what we are really like, they won't like us. Large size is not the only protective device. Small size works too.

From Responsibility

We could use a slight and slender frame for protection. Staying little can be our decision not to grow up. We can use small size and appropriate body language and words in order to invite folks to take care of us and protect us. In this way, we believe we are protecting ourselves from responsibility for ourselves, for getting our needs met, or for facing the consequences of our decisions.

POWER

Power and size are associated in our culture. In the last 50 years, with only the exception of Harry Truman, each United States President has been a relatively tall man. Golda Meir, Eleanor Roosevelt, Margaret Thatcher, and Queen Elizabeth II have been tall or of sturdy build. There is a statistically significant number of tall men in the top echelon of big business. Large people literally and figuratively stand over the rest of the population.

Angela Barron McBride, associate professor and assistant chairman of the Department of Psychiatric and Mental-Health Nursing at the Indiana School of Nursing, affirms that abundant size has long been considered an indication of strength and capability in a woman and that this characteristic is considered at odds with beauty.[2]

Susan is an effective, high-level executive. Although she is enjoying renewed confidence and vigor which accompany her change from destructive to healthy eating patterns, she has choosen to remain heavy. "As the only female on our board, I have enough trouble convincing the men that what I have to say is important. I'm afraid if I were smaller, they would be even more patronizing than they already are and treat me like an empty-headed bit of fluff."

Jim is currently overweight. After an unsuccessful struggle to regain the slight frame of his youth, Jim admitted that he actually prefers being husky. He feels comfortable and powerful—more confident. He thinks that other powerful people pay more attention to him when he is heavier. Keeping extra body weight as a symbol of strength or power is a valid choice. Others have made a different choice.

Charles embarked on a program of running, working out, and healthy eating. As he got his body in better shape, he felt stronger and more powerful. He no longer needed to be larger to feel like a "take-charge" person.

Louise cultivated a businesslike demeanor and appearance. She learned to speak in a manner which clearly communicated that she expected to be heard. After she achieved the desired results, she felt secure enough to let go of the power conveyed by her size.

THE DECISION IS YOURS

You may choose to maintain your body size because the purpose it serves for you is still a viable one, or you may have recognized your hidden agenda in this chapter and be ready to update it or to find the time and help necessary to work through the issues you've uncovered. Whatever your decision regarding size, I invite you to begin a recovery program of self-care and healthy eating.

NOTES

1. William Bennett and Joel Gurin, *The Dieter's Dilemma.* (New York: Basic Books, Inc., 1982), p. 6.
2. Nadine Brozan, Angela Barron McBride Interview, *The Minneapolis Tribune,* March 30, 1980, p. 17F.

IV

GETTING WELL: CHANGING LIFESTYLES

10
Changing Self-Criticism to Self-Care

We Foodaholics have many outstanding qualities. Most of us like people. We really *care* about others and we do lots of nice things to help make them comfortable and happy. Many of us even have caretaker jobs: teaching, day care or health care provision, secretarial, parenting. Our caretaker responsibilities may have begun early in life when we decided it was our job to take care of our parents or siblings. (See Chapter 6, The Foodaholic Family System.)

We do a fine job of meeting the needs of others. We have finely tuned antennae that pick up the feelings of others. Folks rarely have to even ask us for what they want. Even less often do we refuse them.

We have a lot to offer and a lot to give. Sometimes we give it all, and then some, and then more. We're excellent caretakers of our bosses, spouses, children, parents, friends, neighbors, co-workers, plants and pets. You may be thinking to yourself: "What nice unselfish folks we are. What could possibly be wrong with these human qualities of caring and giving?"

Nothing, unless we feel shortchanged: "After all I've done for them, you'd think they'd do what I ask just this once." Unless we feel resentful and notice: "There's never any time left for me to do what I want or to

take decent care of myself." Or unless we give much more than we get and end up feeling used and depleted.

Imagine that it is late at night, and we've spent our time, energy, and motivation focusing on other folks: their wants, their thoughts, their needs, their feelings, their priorities, their activities. We've given them prime time and top importance. So now, what is left for us? The dregs! Time has run out; we feel run down. Our input circuits are overloaded and our reservoir has dried up. We who are so giving have nothing left to give ourselves.

What is our handy solution to the problem? We eat! We stuff ourselves with "goodies" to substitute for the commodities we really want: free time, fun, love, relaxation, rest, physical activity, rewards, and caring from others.

We who have nurtured others so well offer ourselves our personalized version of caretaking. We say to ourselves:

- "Gee, your energy is really low. You need some energy food." (Meaning sweets.)
- "Those leftovers look appealing. Go ahead and eat them. You deserve it."
- "You seem depressed. Another piece of pie will help you feel better."
- "Oh, you poor thing, you've had such a tough day. Have another helping." (Do we substitute another helping for the help we don't request?)

Would I offer only this kind of nurturing to those I care about? My children? My clients? My friends? No way! These invitations to eat destructively sound disgusting!

These messages inside my head used to sound sweet and caring.

When I evaluated them, I realized that I was a crummy caretaker of myself. I was offering myself "sticky, patronizing and destructive"[1] nurturing—marshmallowing. Jean I. Clarke, author of *Self Esteem: A Family Affair*, describes a Marshmallow Caretaker as someone who "blames other people, situations or fate: 'You poor thing. You must have had a bad/lucky break' . . . 'There's nothing you can do.'" Marshmallowing "enables self-destructive behavior and leads a person to wish for magic . . . carries the other person's burden or invites a person to be responsible for other people's feelings."[2]

I now feel angry about the junky food and marshmallow nurturing I used to feed myself. There was little nourishment in either the food or my caretaking. By comparing notes with others, I have discovered that this sweet, destructive nurturing is the Voice of Addiction. It is this voice which says: "Take whatever you need to feel better." For some people the "whatever" is alcohol, for others drugs; for me it was food.

My marshmallowing Voice of Addiction had an endless list of "special occasions"—times when I gave myself permission to indulge in abusive eating. How many of these invitations to binge are blessed by your marshmallow messages?

- Thanksgiving
- Christmas or Chanukah
- New Year's Eve
- Halloween
- Valentine's Day
- Mother's/Father's Day
- Easter
- Fourth of July
- Labor Day
- Memorial Day
- Vacation
- House guests
- My birthday
- Relative's birthday (how many?)
- Friend's birthday (how many?)
- Coworker's birthday (how many?)
- Neighbor's birthday (how many?)
- Boss's birthday
- Acquaintance's birthday (how many?)

- Anniversary of friends
    - parents
    - ours
    - the bank
    - the supermarket   ⎫
    - local restaurant   ⎬   free cake
    - movie theatre   ⎭   and punch
    - department store

- Add your own: _____

_____

Count the invitations. How many special occasions for destructive eating are on your list? _____. In the future, as you become aware of more and more occasions that you use for abusive eating, add them to your list. Has the sheer weight of numbers convinced you that you are self-nurturing as a Marshmallow instead of a healthy Caretaker?

Another distinct voice in our internal dialogue is the Resident Critic. We berate ourselves:

- You slob, your clothes fit terribly!
- You made a pig of yourself—again!
- I can't trust you around food at all.
- You are disgusting.
- You should be ashamed of yourself.
- Feel guilty!

Sometimes we can almost hear our Marshmallower and Critic arguing with each other. The Critic might motivate us to "shape-up" temporarily, until we tire of trying to meet our exacting perfectionist demands and rebel with another binge, encouraged by the Marshmallower. Although the rigid diet structure imposed by the Critic may initially feel comforting, it makes little difference who wins; neither one helps us recover, over the long haul, from our eating disorder or obsession with food.

Our recovery lies in using our talent and strength as caretakers in our own behalf. Those wonderfully effective antennae that sense so well the needs of others can be retracted and focused inward to help us direct our own well-developed nurturing skills toward ourselves.

THERE'S A LITTLE PERSON INSIDE MY HEAD THAT TELLS ME RIGHT FROM WRONG. SHE'S MY RESIDENT CRITIC.

WHEN I OVERINDULGE SHE SCOLDS ME, WHEN I GET ANGRY, SHE SHAMES ME, WHEN I SAY "NO", SHE GUILTS ME......

IF I'M CONSTANTLY PERFECT, SHE WILL PRAISE ME!

IF I DON'T ANNIHILATE HER FIRST!!

In our Foodaholic classes and workshops, this exercise is offered to enhance self-nurturing skills and tone down marshmallowing and criticizing voices. I suggest you read this fantasy exercise in a gentle voice as you tape record it for yourself. Or you could ask someone to read it to you or tape it for you. Or you could send for the taped version.[3] As you read the fantasy, pause about 10 seconds for each dash. If you choose not to work with a tape, and simply read the fantasy, allow yourself time to picture and experience each part.

Trust yourself. Respond to the fantasy as you wish. If you feel sleepy, let yourself drift off. You will still hear what you need to hear. If in your fantasy you veer off in a different direction, do it your way. If you find it difficult to relax, simply notice that and let it be. As a general rule, the harder you *try* to relax, the more tense you will become. Just remain quiet, and keep bringing your mind gently back from your busy thoughts to the fantasy exercise.

CARETAKER FANTASY

Make your body as comfortable as possible. Close your eyes and begin to breathe deeply.... Feel the energy and relaxation enter your body as you inhale, and picture your tension draining out as you exhale.... Now you can relax your body deeply and completely, starting with your toes. Imagine that your breath is entering through your toes, and brings with it relaxation.... Pay attention to your feet and ankles. Let the relaxation enter your feet and ankles. Let them be so relaxed, it's almost like floating.... Let the relaxation travel up through your calves, your knees, and your thighs. Your legs feel light and melting.... Let your bottom and your genitals feel relaxed and floating too.... Send your breath into your stomach, and with it relaxation and a sense of well-being. Feel how light and floating your stomach is.... Let the warm relaxation creep through your chest and back. . . . Let go of the tension in your shoulders and neck. Feel the spreading warmth and relaxation. . . . Let that lovely sensation flow slowly down your arms to your fingertips. . . . Now, relax your face: your jaw, your teeth, your tongue, your cheeks, your eyes, your forehead. . . . Let go of the tension in your scalp. Your whole head feels warm and relaxed. . . . Your whole body feels light and floating. . . .

Now, imagine that you are the caretaker of that light, relaxed body. You are a warm, loving person who is usually giving and caring toward other people, and you know how to offer them responsible care. Only now your assignment is focused on your own body. Look at that body with a sense of fondness, of caring. . . . Do not allow yourself to focus on your figure faults, but rather, let yourself appreciate the ways in which your body serves you well. . . . Let yourself know that it is the only body you will have in this life. Value it highly. Respect it. Imagine that you are expressing your caring with your touch. . . .

You, Mr. or Ms. Caretaker, you have a crucial task. The energy, health, and well-being of this body, and its clarity of mind and emotional stability, depend on you. With your good advice, wise decisions, and gentle caring, this fine body will continue to serve you long and well. Not only that, but with your increased concern and help, it will grow healthier and more energetic than ever. Picture how it will be. . . .

You, the caretaker, are in charge. Only you have ultimate power and control over this body. No one else's standards and opinions matter. *You* set the standards for how this body should look and act. You are well-prepared for your role as caretaker. You are intelligent, loving, gentle, and well-informed. You do not exert your power in criticizing or hassling ways, but, instead, by using your wisdom and firmness. You are a Winner! Imagine yourself treating this body exactly as an outstanding caretaker would. . . .

Now, get in touch with your body again. You, Body, you are even more relaxed. You have a sense of being in kind and competent hands. You feel strong and secure because of that. You know that you and your Caretaker are both Winners! Way down in the pit of your stomach you know that. Let yourself feel cared for there in your stomach. Let yourself experience the joy and contentment that result from being so highly valued. . . .

Taste those feelings in your mouth. Feel them on your tongue. . . . You know that your Caretaker will be in charge. S/he will be in charge of when and how you will eat; when and how you will engage in physical activity; and when and how you will relax or have fun. You feel relieved knowing that and you may decide to carry that relaxed feeling around with you from now on. . . .

Let yourself picture the little girl/little boy who still lives within your grownup body. . . . Allow yourself to know that even while you are busy being mature, responsible, and successful, your little one has needs and the right to have them met. . . . So have a dialogue with the Caretaker part of you and ask for whatever you need. Perhaps you need encouragement, support, or permission to do things differently. Maybe you want a pat on the back for how far you've come already. I'll bet you'd like a big hug and some words to let you know you're loved for who you are. You might enjoy being told that you're a neat person at any weight. . . .

Let yourself feel how it is to know that you can depend on your Caretaker, the grown-up part of you, to gently take you by the hand and lead you away from destructive eating to healthy foods. . . . Listen to your Caretaker tell you that s/he will be available to you whenever you have a need. . . . Now do whatever you need to to say good-bye for a little while. . . . Let yourself become gradually and gently more aware of your environment. When you are ready, you may open your eyes. Probably you will feel fully alert and alive, energized, and yet very relaxed.

How did you experience the fantasy exercise?

Was being Caretaker to yourself a whole new sensation?

Did you feel nurturing toward yourself?

Did the Child within you feel relieved, exhilarated, and reassured knowing that a grownup is in charge?

Did you feel sad or forlorn realizing how little nurturing you've received?

Or did you feel anxious about your lack of experience with good self-care? Unable to fantasize? Unable to relax? Other?

Many of us recovering Foodaholics have found it highly beneficial to do this exercise regularly—daily or several times weekly. Problems encountered the first time smooth out with repetition of the exercise so long as we don't hassle ourselves over failure to achieve a specific level of performance.

It is helpful to realize that the Destructive Eater who lurks within each of us is but an impulsive small child. Traditionally we have scolded, berated, and expected that "Kid" part of us to be controlled and discriminating, as if s/he were an adult!

How do we curb a little child who is engaged in acting spontaneously, albeit destructively? Even an adolescent caretaking a sibling or a neighbor child knows enough not to harangue the child to use greater self-control or willpower. A good nurturer diverts the child or sets limits. We know this. We have offered this kind of nurturing for years, to everyone but ourselves!

CARETAKER TECHNIQUES

To strengthen your self-nurturing muscles, figure out alternatives to your destructive eating. Picture yourself taking the little boy/girl that is you by the hand, saying: "Oh, no, honey. That is bad for you. Let's go get ____ instead." Here is a list of ideas for "instead ofs."

do some physical activity
do relaxation techniques
find warm, nurturing friends
get enough sleep
ask for compliments
ask for help
read an enjoyable book or magazine
watch interesting TV
get support
keep a healthy food supply
plan how to handle threatening situations
have fun or play
take some goof-off time
get physical touch
get a massage
shop for clothes
grooming activities:
  manicure
  shampoo
  haircut
shoeshine
facial
make-up demonstration
pedicure
sensual pleasure:
  lie in the sun
  take a bubble bath
  take a long, luxurious shower
  listen to music
  rub your bare feet on the lawn
  watch the clouds
  take a nature walk
  dance
  engage in sexual activity
  relax in a hot tub or sauna
others: _____
  _____
  _____
  _____

ASSIGNMENT

Caretaker techniques are good coping skills for stress reduction, curing food obsession, and working toward high-level wellness. Select from the preceding list *two techniques* that are new for you. Make a contract with yourself for how you will use these methods in caretaking yourself in the next two weeks. Be sure your contract is positive, specific, and attainable.

Not: I will run 5 miles per day. (Haven't run in 6 months!)

Rather: I will run 15 minutes at least three times each week. (You can always increase it when you feel ready.)

Not: I won't overeat on my vacation visit to my parents.

Rather: I will eat three healthy meals and no desserts. I will ask Mom to get interesting fruits and vegetables for my snacks.

Not: I will take more time to relax.

Rather: I will do a relaxation technique, read fiction, or take a nap for at least 20 minutes daily between 5 and 6 P.M. Plus, I will take one morning, afternoon, or evening per week to do only what I want.

Your Contracts

1) _____

2) _____

There are additional ways of strengthening your self-nurturing skills. You can flex your caretaker muscles in your own behalf to be more in touch with the small Child within you and to establish closer contact between your Caretaker and your little person.

Find a stuffed animal, throw pillow, or sweater that reminds you of the Child part of you and take time each day for holding and talking to him or her with lots of caretaker messages:

- You can wiggle your toes and tense, then relax your muscles during long, tedious meetings, instead of feeling trapped and agitated.
- I'm going to take you to bed early tonight. You're too tired to watch TV, and the world won't end if you don't do those chores.

The Child in you might cherish some affirmations:

- You're a neat person.
- I have faith in you.
- You're a winner!

Experiment with giving permissions to yourself or your soft, cuddly stand-in:

- It's okay to goof off and have fun.
- You deserve to enjoy life.
- It's okay for you to say no. You don't have to please everybody.

Another way to contact the Kid within yourself is to pretend that s/he is a foster child who has come to live at your house. To help your Child become acclimated to this new environment, imagine you are explaining what is going on in this house, what you are doing, and why:

- "Now it's teethbrushing time. It prevents cavities and gum disease."
- "Let's go grocery shopping. There aren't any nutritious snacks around here."

You may discover that you are more adept at self-care than you had first thought. Focusing on and making more tangible your internal Caretaker-Child dialogues will broaden and strengthen your self-nurturing skills. Such skills are essential as you go on to divorce yourself from the Foodaholic system.

NOTES

1. Jean Illsley Clarke, *Self-Esteem: A Family Affair.* (Minneapolis, MN: Winston Press, 1978), pp. 268–269.
2. *Ibid.*
3. Foodaholics' Treatment Center, 7250 France Avenue South, Minneapolis, MN, 55435. Cost is $10.00.

11

Divorcing Ourselves from the Foodaholic System

Making a sincere effort to recover from our food obsession while at the same time retaining our roles in the sick family or social system is akin to butting our heads against a brick wall. The attempt to change other people in the system is an equally hopeless task. There are, however, some constructive steps which we can take to separate ourselves from the destructive elements of the Foodaholic family and society.

DISCHARGING OUR JURY
AND HELPERS

Inevitably, as part of our eating disorder, we Foodaholics have one or more relationships in which our size, weight, food consumption, or dieting are frequently commented upon, questioned, judged, and evaluated:

- Gaining weight there, aren't you?
- You should try this new diet.
- You don't need that second helping.

- What did you have to eat today?
- How much did you weigh this morning?
- Did you stay on your diet?
- How much have you lost?
- That's not on your diet.
- I thought you were worried about gaining weight.

It is irrelevant whether our judges and jury are self-designated or we have invited them into roles of judging us with our constant self-criticism. It is no longer important whether these people are actually being as helpful as they think they are or whether they are a hindrance. No longer does it matter that these people relate to us in a judgmental way because we allow them to do so. What *is* important is that we fire them from their roles. Now. Unless we do fire them, we cannot learn to assume direct responsibility for our bodies. We are involved in a relationship triangle in which we and others in our system take these roles: Victim, Rescuer, and Persecutor. These roles comprise the Drama Triangle, as originated by Dr. Stephen Karpman.[1] The Drama Triangle provides a graphic illustration of the roles and moves in the psychological games people play. Once we have assumed one of the roles with its accompanying emotions, we are likely to get involved in the psychological "game" and experience all three roles on the triangle, with their accompanying emotions.

It is possible to play games, to take all positions on the triangle in our own internal dialogue, particularly when we use external things such as food, a diet, or body size to take one of the roles.

The Victim role is played by a one-down person who experiences feelings of helplessness, inadequacy, and self-pity. Victims typically see themselves as ineffective, failing, stupid, or ugly. The Victim searches for a Rescuer but also invites persecution with downtrodden expressions.

The Rescuer is a one-up role. The Rescuer feels needed, important, smart, or helpful. The Rescuer believes the Victim to be inadequate and unable to manage without help. The Rescuer usually (1) thinks for the Victim; (2) helps without being specifically asked; (3) does more than 50 percent of the problem-solving work; (4) helps even when s/he would prefer not to; and (5) repeatedly does things for the Victim that the person is capable of doing for him/herself. The existence of any three of these conditions clearly indicates a rescue operation.

The Persecutor is also in a one-up role. The Persecutor feels or acts overtly or covertly angry, is aggressive, intrusive, or judgmental toward the

Victim. The Persecutor imposes his/her values, expectations, or "shoulds" on the Victim. The Persecutor may also criticize the Rescuer for helping. That is one means by which Rescuers may, in turn, experience the Victim Role. Also, Rescuers are victimized by neglecting their own needs or by taking on an excessive burden in order to meet the needs of the Victim.

In his book, *Games People Play*,[2] Dr. Eric Berne describes a number of emotionally painful interactions he identifies as psychological games. Following is a list of games that Foodaholics play, accompanied by the descriptive labels Dr. Berne developed for them:

Wooden Leg
Rapo
Kick Me
Ain't It Awful (AIA)
Now I've Got You, You SOB (NIGYSOB)
Do Me Something
See What You Made Me Do
If It Weren't For You (IWFY)
I'm Only Trying to Help You (ITHY)
Blemish

To this list I would like to add another game which I call Poor Little Me or PLM. For a more extensive description of the dynamics of these self-defeating interactions, refer to *Games People Play*.

The following examples illustrate how our statements and thoughts and those of others fit a specific position on the triangle. The powers with which we endow our food, diet, or body are reflected in the "statements" attributed to them and their positions on the triangle. The game(s) being played is/are in parentheses.

V = Me: I feel victimized. I am helpless about food. (Wooden Leg, PLM)
P = Food: One won't hurt—ha, ha, and then: I get you every time. (Rapo, NIGYSOB)
R = Other: Just try this diet. Or but that's not on your diet. (ITHY)

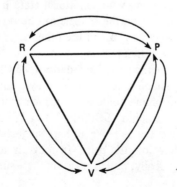

P = Other:	What did you eat today?
	What did you weigh this morning? (sounds concerned, helpful and Rescuing but is really being aggressive and persecuting.) (NIGYSOB and Blemish)
V = Me:	Gulp! I'll have to confess or lie. (Kick Me)
R = Food:	There, there, don't feel bad. You'll feel better if you eat. (ITHY and Rapo)
V = Other:	I'm so embarrassed when my friends see how much weight you've gained. (Kick Me, IWFY, PLM, Do Me Something)
P = My Body:	(to Other) Now I've Gotcha. I can make you feel bad. (NIGYSOB)
R = Me:	(to Other) Don't worry, I'll cut down to 500 calories daily. (Thus becoming the next Victim) (Look How Hard I've Tried, Kick Me)
P = Me:	(to my Body) I hate you. You're ugly. (Blemish, Kick Me)
V = My Body:	You're right. Poor me. Nobody likes a fat person. (PLM, Kick Me)
R = Other:	Now if you'll just cut out second helpings and eating between meals . . . (Implied message is Persecutor: You're right. Nobody likes you the way you are.) (ITHY)
V = Me:	I blew it. I fell off my diet last night. I never can do it right. (Kick Me, PLM, Wooden Leg)
P = Diet:	I am impossible to stay on. You failure. (NIGYSOB)
R = Other:	I know how you feel. It's so hard to stay on a diet, particularly with all the fattening stuff they serve around here. (Ain't it awful? Invitation to play Wooden Leg)

Think about one relationship you have with others in which food, size, and dieting are often discussed. Diagram your roles on the Triangle. Then map out the moves, noting your emotional state in each position. The roles taken and the moves on the triangle can be very subtle. You will be able to infer what positions you and the other person take from how you feel after interacting with that person.

In order to strengthen our boundaries (See Chapter 6, Foodaholic Family System) and establish our jurisdiction over our own bodies and our food and in order to remove some of the game-playing elements from our relationships, we can establish "Beltlines."[3] In a boxing match it is against the rules to hit below the belt. We all have subjects about which we are sensitive, which "hit below the belt." In a caring relationship we often agree, implicitly or verbally, not to mention these subjects. We know how to establish taboos out of consideration for others' feelings or to protect ourselves from their negative reactions.

In order to separate from a Foodaholic system that is perpetuating our food problems, we can actively proceed to establish and enforce Beltlines. Changing the impact the system has on us is crucial. Whether or not we aided and abetted our own victimization is no longer relevant. We need to drop or change our previous role in the system.

The following are some examples of beltline-setting statements.

- I'm not going to talk about that anymore. It's part of my recovery program. (I invite us to stay off the triangle by not engaging in our former roles.)
- I would like an agreement that in our relationship we not talk about _____. I think it will improve our relationship. Are you willing? (I do not want us to continue in our old roles.)
- You say that you are concerned about me. Well, if you are, you will not bring up _____ because your doing so is painful for me. (Stop persecuting.)
- I appreciate your concern about _____. However, it is not helpful. This is my problem, and I am handling it in my own way. (Stop rescuing.)
- It is my body. No matter how hard you try, you cannot live in it or control it. (Stop imposing yourself.)
- I am not willing to discuss this subject any longer. (I will not be victimized.)
- I have told you before, your comments are unwelcome. (I will not be victimized.)
- I feel angry when you set yourself up as judge and jury whose jurisdiction includes what I eat or how I look. I will be my own judge. (Stop persecuting.)
- I want you to stop right now.
- Stop!
- Get off my back.
- Bug off!

The statements are listed in approximate order of increasing assertiveness. I invite you to start with milder requests and the reminders that will probably be necessary. If other people persistently impose their comments and opinions, invading the territory you have declared to be off limits, you will be obliged to increase the directness of your requests.

TURNING FOOD BUDDIES
INTO FRIENDS

Many alcoholics choose to surround themselves with drinking buddies in order to have an excuse as well as supportive companionship for their drinking. So, too, do many Foodaholics have buddies—our "food buddies." We constantly talk about food, weight and dieting with these special people. We enthusiastically exchange recipes and restaurant reviews. Eating or simply planning a food-centered event are probably favorite leisure time activities. Our recreation, communication and socialization activities systematically revolve around food as well as formal and informal opportunities for eating.

In order to relegate food to a less pivotal role in our lives, it is important that we first stop discussing it, so that we can direct our positive energy toward other subjects and behaviors.

Make a list of the folks with whom you discuss food, restaurants, weight, dieting, or recipes. Under each name list at least four alternative subjects of conversation with that person.

1. (name of person) _____   2. _____

   a. _____   a. _____

   b. _____   b. _____

   c. _____   c. _____

   d. _____   d. _____

3. _____   4. _____

   a. _____   a. _____

   b. _____   b. _____

   c. _____   c. _____

   d. _____   d. _____

The next time the food talk starts, switch to one of your optional subjects. You might discover that some of your Food Buddies are not so easily dissuaded from their familiar "foodalogues." If so, you will need to inform them that you are turning over a new leaf, that you value your relationship and that your goal is to explore other interesting conversation and activities together. If your Food Buddy persists in speaking of food, you may want to establish a beltline.

SAYING NO

Saying no is an essential tool for recovery because it helps us set limits and strengthen our boundaries, and it is an important method of caretaking ourselves. It aids in differentiating between our own and others' problems, preferences, priorities, needs, work, and time, so that we can avoid caretaking others to the detriment of our own self-care.

Selfishness is not a sin; it is a survival skill, a facilitator for our growth. Every infant is born selfish. We can't get what we want any other way. Some of us are socialized or shamed out of our selfishness earlier or to a greater extent than others. When we say no to others and they accuse us of being insensitive or selfish, that is not the insult they think it is— actually, it is a compliment! It means we are interested in improving our quality of life, growing as a person, and taking action to meet our needs. Those who object to our new self-care skills may actually be competing with us over who gets to be "selfish."

When saying no is a new behavior for us, we need to be prepared to continue in spite of our guilt feelings or the negative reactions of those disappointed others. Perhaps we have been handling their problems, work, ways of living, values, feelings, and emotions, and in other ways taking responsibility for them. It is only natural that they feel disappointed. They are not bad people, although they may, at times, become vindictive or angry in an effort to pull or push us back into our old familiar caretaker role. We, too, would not cheerfully nor passively relinquish all that caretaking. We might use every trick we could think of to keep someone doing those things for us. Recognizing that they are working hard to pull us back into old roles helps us avoid feeling guilty when they are angry.

We probably do not want to stop being genuinely warm and caring people. We do not want to shut others out of our lives. We will meet their needs and our responsibilities as we choose. There are some questions we can ask ourselves to help in setting guidelines for saying no or yes to others.

- Do I believe this is my responsibility or does someone else think that?
- Have I been asked to do something specific?

- By choosing this responsibility will I be, in fact, confirming to that person that s/he is helpless or inadequate?
- Will I be doing more than 50 percent of the work in handling the other person's problem?
- Is my taking charge in this situation enabling someone else to remain passive?
- Do I want to say no to this request or imposition?
- If I say yes, will I feel resentful (Persecutor) or reluctant and overwhelmed (Victim)?
- Will becoming involved or helping another force me to neglect my self-care or put me in a stressful or uncomfortable position (Victim)?

Affirmative answers to any of the above questions are indications that we are Rescuing, not Caretaking. Diminishing or discounting another in the guise of helpfulness is harmful. It can best be determined, especially when working with children, the handicapped, or the elderly, by answering the question: Am I doing for this person something s/he is capable of doing for her/himself?

As a caring, giving person, I am willing occasionally to tie shoelaces for a tired child, run errands for a friend, or help a family member or coworker write a report, even though he or she usually is capable of managing without my help. But if the child often whines in order to get shoelace-tying, if my friend is frequently harried and wants more than occasional errand-running, or if my coworker will not complete a report without my assistance, then my helpfulness may be crippling to them.

To refuse them is to practice the gentle art of Selective Neglect.[4] That means we give them credit for being able to meet their own needs and for being good problem-solvers, no matter how strongly they protest that they really aren't. We can still remain flexible and make exceptions when they are sick, or tired, or truly cannot do some things for themselves.

Another skill to help avoid rescuing is called the Principle of Accountability. This is a high-sounding phrase that simply asks the question: "Whose problem is it?" We may be relieved to realize it is the other person's problem. It is not a joint problem. It is not ours alone. At this point we can ask ourselves: "Am I willing to be involved in the solution?" If our answer is "no," we will do neither ourselves nor the other a favor by saying "yes" and giving another the dubious benefit of our reluctant or resentful attention. We could be setting ourselves up on the Drama Triangle, first as Rescuer and ultimately as Victim or Persecutor.

If we decide that we are willing to be involved we can use an important skill to keep out of the Rescuer role. The skill is called a Request for a Statement of Needs and asks the other person any of the following questions:

- What can I do that would be helpful?
- What do you need right now?
- What would be most useful to you?
- What do you want me to do?

By employing this skill of encouraging others to ask for what they want, we are helping instead of Rescuing. We are encouraging people to be assertive. We are avoiding doing their thinking. We are allowing others to remain in charge of their needs instead of leaping in feet first to Rescue them.

"No" is a nice, big, strong word. It can stand alone; it need not be supported by excuses, explanations, or embellishments. When we choose to offer a reason for our refusal, we can protect ourselves by keeping it brief and not allowing it to be discounted. A paragraph of explanation could indicate that we are trying to convince ourselves and others that it is okay for us to refuse. This clue to our uncertainty could encourage others to manipulate us. It is also helpful when we recognize that a person is determined to nullify our reasons for refusing (example: door-to-door salesperson or a child who won't take no for an answer). In the interests of self-care, we need not bother to offer reasons that will only be denied or used against us. Our no's can stand alone and are the stronger for doing so.

Some people see rejection lurking around every corner. Turning a kind refusal into a cruel rejection is a switch they make in their own internal dialogue. It is not our responsibility to protect them from their own imagination. It is not our responsibility to say "yes" just so they won't feel rejected.

One method of refusing kindly is called the Yes-No Response. With this technique I can say "yes" to the person and avoid rejecting him or her while saying "no" to the request. A list of yes and no responses follow. The object is to first make a statement from Column A, and then one from column B.

A	B
Yes to the Person	*No to the Request*
I have faith in you.	I have other priorities, other commitments.
I care about you.	
You're entitled to ...	It's against my values.
I think you're capable.	It's important to me that ...

A (continued)	B (continued)
Yes to the Person	*No to the Request*
You solve problems well (give example when possible).	I will not; am not willing.
	I choose not to.
You know what works best for you.	I've decided not to.
	I'm not going to.
I like you.	I have other needs.
You're neat.	It is uncomfortable for me.
You're fun.	I don't like to.
I like being with you.	It doesn't feel good for me.
	I have problems of my own to take care of.
	I have as much as I can handle.
	I don't want to.

I prefer to keep my yes statement and no statement clearly separate. I can achieve that by using short sentences or by choosing "and" as the word between the yes statement and the no statement. I avoid using but. When I say: "I like you, but . . ." it has the effect of wiping out or diminishing my positive statement. Using the conjunction "and" felt awkward to me at first, yet other people did not seem to notice.

I can, if I choose, add a third part to my statement. I can add what I am willing to do instead. The following examples contain: (a) the yes statement, (b) the no statement, and (c) the instead of statement:

(a) "You are a very capable person. I have seen you pack a great lunch for yourself, and (b) I am not willing to pack it for you. (c) I will write a list of possible menus to give you some ideas."

(a) "I care a great deal about you and hate to see you so unhappy. (b) I am uncomfortable being involved in this problem between two people I like. (c) How about a big hug instead?"

If we evade a direct yes or no answer with: "I'm too busy now" or "I don't have time," we are secretly hoping the problem will be handled without our involvement. We are being neither direct nor self-nurturing. Our delaying tactics may ultimately place us in the Victim role. At first we may feel uncomfortable with a direct no. It is ultimately more respectful of ourselves and others.

For those occasions when others who want something from us discount the reasons we offer for refusing or badger, corner, push, or prod us, we can learn to respond with a quiet, firm "I don't want to." "I don't want to" stands alone. It requires no support, no excuses, no explanations. Only we know what we do or don't want to do, and others' wheedling, persuading, or convincing will have little impact on our real preferences. We have a right to refuse in this way. We are not bad people for doing so.

FEELING AND THINKING

We Foodaholics tend to think and act as if experiencing our emotions were bad. We seek to avoid our feelings by stuffing them down or by sedating them either with lots of food or the kinds of food that cause us to feel lethargic. We tell ourselves and others that eating makes us happy. But, at best, the pleasure we feel pales in comparison to the real pleasures of an active, nonaddictive life. To the extent that we succeed in numbing our negative emotions, we also succeed in numbing ourselves to positive emotions. When we believe in an all or nothing myth about emotions, our fears and actions based on this belief have the power of turning myth into reality.

Sadness

Frequently we measure, judge, label, and limit our sadness. While acknowledging that some circumstances are genuinely painful, we still attempt to restrain, ignore, or tranquilize emotion. If our sadness persists or is too intense, we add the label self-pity. Then we try even *harder* to talk ourselves out of our feeling of sadness and we criticize ourselves more for being weak or emotional.

We may actually feel guilty when we exceed the prescribed amount of sadness, which—since we deal in mythical quantities—we can call one cupful. Instead of accepting the fact that our sadness is, right now, greater —ten gallons maybe or even half a ton—we scare ourselves by imagining that if we allow ourselves to start crying, we will never stop and we'll descend into some bottomless pit of sadness, never to return. We are afraid to admit to our vulnerability and our need for caretaking. Who decides how much emotion is too much? Who evaluates your sadness?

In order to let go of sadness, we must allow ourselves to feel sad for as long as we need to, to cry if we feel like it, to ask for hugs, holding, and help, and in the process, be permissive, understanding Caretakers to ourselves.

Fear

When we feel frightened about something, we often proceed to terrify ourselves further, using the fear itself! We tell ourselves how awful it is that we are anxious or fearful. We may predict that we will be incapacitated, or less effective if we allow ourselves to acknowledge and experience our fear. Fearing inadequacy in addition to feeling afraid, we head for our familiar anesthesia, food. Sometimes we wonder why we so frequently feel hungry. We don't realize that anxiety can cause the same discomfort or sense of emptiness in the pit of our stomach as hunger does.

It is not a weakness to feel fear. On the contrary, it takes a courageous person to admit it. And one *can* be scared and still achieve a lot. It is a myth that feeling afraid eliminates our taking action. Admitting that we are afraid can help us to move through and beyond our fear to accomplish that which we fear. Sometimes, by getting more information, rehearsing an action scene, or by carefully structuring the situation, we can provide the margin of comfort we need.

Anger

We probably believe more mythology around anger than any other emotion. We tell ourselves our anger cannot be trusted, that it is not safe for us to feel angry. When we feel like hitting someone or exploding with anger and fantasize harming or eliminating someone we criticize even our fantasies and tell ourselves that we are violent people. We confuse fantasy with reality. If wishes could kill, we'd all be dead!

As little children, we experienced an emotion and acted upon it almost simultaneously. It is likely that others reacted negatively to some of the ways in which we expressed our anger. As children we concluded that our angry feeling itself was bad. There are no "bad" feelings. All emotions are okay. Some are more pleasant than others, but they are all acceptable.

As grownups, we can decide how to act or not to act upon our emotions. Our Caretaker can set limits and make responsible choices. For instance: It is okay to feel angry; it is okay to express anger; it is not okay to cause harm to others, property, or ourselves. My good Caretaker decides when and how it is safe for me to express my anger.

Verbal expression of anger can be directed toward the person or situation involved in a non-abusive way, or can be indirect, such as when we ask an uninvolved person to listen for a few minutes while we get it off our chest. We can use physical expression to release anger from our bodies by stomping up some steps, slamming drawers or doors, kicking pillows, yelling in the shower or the car, shadowboxing, growling, cursing, or slamming a ball in a game of tennis, raquetball, or soccer.

Sexuality

Stuffing ourselves with food can easily confuse and diminish our sexual feelings. We may attempt to hide our attractiveness with excess flesh. We scare ourselves into thinking that once we allow ourselves to feel sexy, we will become promiscuous or unfaithful. We assume that if people approach us longingly, then we are doomed. We confuse the wanting, theirs or ours, with the getting.

We can say no to someone who makes a pass or acts seductively. We can briskly inform someone we don't like how he or she is behaving toward us. We are not responsible for others' sexual feelings toward us, unless we have been acting seductively. Even then, they are still responsible for their behavior; we are not.

So, too, can we choose how we will act upon our own sexual feelings. We can experience them, find pleasure in them, and still decide not to act upon them. The mere existence of a sexual feeling does not mean we are "loose," sinful, nondiscriminating, or an animal. The emotions are okay, as are any lurid fantasies in which we may indulge. We don't have to follow through on either one.

Boredom

Eating is not a cure for boredom. If we allow ourselves to live with our occasional feelings of boredom it will simply run its course. Either we will get bored with being bored, stop boring ourselves, and become good, interesting company or we will explore new ways to build a more interesting lifestyle. We cannot be experiencing excitement or interest constantly. Some of us simply label the lull between excitements as boredom. We need to accept those lulls and quiet times as inevitable, as golden opportunities to assimilate and integrate information and experiences.

Guilt

Sometimes, when we are in the process of changing behaviors, or when others tell us we should be feeling or acting in other ways, we feel guilty. We might feel guilty the first few times we say "no" or stand up for ourselves.

Guilt is a learned emotion. It is not innate. Imagine these expressions on the face of a six-month-old infant: anger, fear, sadness, joy, and guilt. Are you having trouble picturing a guilty infant? Guilt and shame are emotions that are taught. For some of us, guilt is pervasive; we have learned our lessons all too well. Nevertheless, it is more possible to refuse to feel guilt because it is learned rather than innate and because it occurs later in our development. There is a greater element of choice in whether or not we will feel guilty.

Our feeling guilty does not mean we have to stop the behavior that provokes it. We can either continue to feel guilty and do it anyway, or we can choose to do it guilt-free. Many of us have the work ethic so strongly ingrained that when we take time to rest, relax, or have fun, we think we are committing a horrible sin. We could "waste" time, as our Resident Critic would term it, while feeling guilty, or take a guilt-free time-out. Our Caretaker can give us permission and tell us we deserve some time for ourselves.

Hunger

Many of us eat preventively to avoid experiencing the feeling of hunger. Perhaps we have chosen to avoid feeling hungry as a consequence of some experience when we were without food for a very long time. Perhaps someone taught us that feeling hungry was bad.

Hunger is a natural human feeling. It is interesting to note the ways that people differ in experiencing hunger. We can feel a variety of sensations in several different places in our bodies. Feeling hungry makes food taste absolutely delicious. It adds to the pleasure of eating. We need not fear being hungry for a little while. Our Caretaker can reassure us there is food available.

Pleasure

Some of us believe that pleasure is rationed. If we get too much, something awful might happen. That is one reason why we sabotage our excitement about achieving our goals and having healthier lives, eating patterns, and bodies. If we get too many compliments, we toss them away or feel embarrassed because we think we don't deserve all that pleasure. We gobble our food hurriedly because if we hardly taste it or fail to enjoy it, we think it counts less. We are afraid that if we thoroughly enjoy ourselves, with food, fun, or sex, we will go out of control and never stop.

We can seek and have pleasure in generous supply. It need not be earned. While it is true that *constant* pleasure-seeking can become boring, aimless, and superficial, we do not need to suffer in order to prove our worth. Finding pleasure in our work is highly motivating and leads to success. I find that taking pleasure in my eating is more satisfying, and thus I need less food. Pleasurable physical activity and relaxation promotes good mental health and enhances emotional stability.

The next chapter, Life Beyond Eating, will further explore ways of living a full and pleasurable life.

NOTES

1. Dr. Stephen B. Karpman, "Fairy Tales and Script Drama Analysis." *Transactional Analysis Bulletin,* Vol. 7, No. *25,* January 1968.
2. Dr. Eric Berne, *Games People Play.* (New York: Ballantine Books, 1964).
3. George R. Bach and Herb Goldberg, *Creative Aggression.* (New York: Doubleday and Company, Inc., 1974), p. 178.
4. Sandra Gordon Stoltz, *Be Your Own Santa Claus.* (Minneapolis, MN: Pathfinder Publications, 1978), pp. 15–16.

12
Life Beyond Eating

Typically, we Foodaholics withhold from ourselves many of the good, desirable things in life. This kind of self-denial could be attributed to many aspects of our thinking and development. We may focus primarily on caretaking others, having been taught that it is selfish to focus on ourselves. Or, we may choose to invest little time or energy in our own self-care because we have doubts that we are deserving, or have the notion that we are entitled to life's benefits only when we have the "correct" appearance or behavior.

We consistently deny or ignore the little boy or girl deep within us. In the interest of performing adequately in society and the world of work, as well as meeting the needs of other folks, we push aside our own needs. As a consequence, the needy Kid inside us grabs what *is* available—food. In fact, eating is one of the few pleasures we allow ourselves to indulge in.

Our food needs will diminish to the extent that we indulge our little one by providing lots of the non-food benefits to which we are entitled, no matter how we look or eat.

TURNING UNTILS INTO NOWS

One of the most blatant and obvious ways we Foodaholics keep ourselves forever yearning and dissatisfied is repeatedly to tell ourselves we may not have x, y, or z *until* we reach a given weight, remain on a rigid diet or exercise regimen, or fit into a certain garment. Meanwhile, the little Kid part of us grows impatient at forever being told "No, wait," or "not until," and finds the one commodity she/he can have now—food. Some of the more common examples of enjoyments we withhold are:

- New clothes until we reach a certain size.
- Swimming or biking because we have negative pictures of how we look in a bathing suit or on a bicycle seat.
- Contacting "fuzzy friends"—cheerful, positive people with whom we feel good, because we want to hide our weight gain from them.

Put an (*X*) in front of any of the items which apply to you. Add your own "untils" to the list: _____

_____

_____

_____

We are entitled to feel proud of the way we are dressed, to engage in physical activities we enjoy, and to relate to people who feel replenishing to us. These feelings and activities are not earned privileges, they are simply the fundamental joys of life. Think about the many ways that you can bring good things into your life. Select one "until" and transform it into a "now" *this week*. Then decide what you will plan next week. Following are examples of "until" to "now" contracts made in Foodaholics' class:

- I will call a longtime friend and arrange to get together with her this weekend. I will not refer to my weight gain.
- I will take my bike to the repair shop. After it is repaired I will ride at least every other day.
- I will buy two new pairs of slacks so I can feel good about how I look *now*.
- I will add to my savings this month and buy myself a stationary cycle next month.

- I will take at least one college course this fall, no matter what my body size. This week I will send for catalogs and registration forms. Within a year, I will enroll in a degree program.
- I will wear shorts outside this weekend.
- I will buy a bathing suit in my current size and then go swimming twice next weekend.
- I will run in the park instead of hiding on back roads.

Now write your contracts:

This week I will _____

Next week I will _____

REWARDS FOR BEING

Most of us Foodaholics think of specific foods as special treats. We reward ourselves with food when we are tired, when we have had a tough day, when we feel deprived, when we want to procrastinate or avoid something.

Make a list of non-food items that seem like special rewards or treats to you:

_____   _____

_____   _____

_____   _____

_____

If you had difficulty writing your list of rewards, that is important information. You may be so out of practice in rewarding yourself with nonfood treats that you no longer know how. To inspire you, here is a list compiled by participants in a Foodaholics' Treatment Program:

massage	flowers
new clothes	facial
books	manicure
magazines	bubble bath
naughty novel	sexual fantasy

daydream
take a class
rub lotion/oil on body
listen to music
wallow in a down comforter
hug a teddy bear
do-whatever-I-want time
buy nonfood treats:
    toys
    a mug
    house decoration
    teddy bear

make a date
go to bed early
cosmetics or perfume
guilt-free time off
take a nap
call a fuzzy friend
play with a pet
cuddling, nuzzling
add yours:

_____

_____

_____

Select two ways in which you will reward yourself this week. These are unearned rewards. You do not have to perform to deserve them. You have already earned them by being you. Contract: I will _____

and _____

FUN AND PLAY

I invite you to make another list. This time make a list of activities that are fun for you or feel like play. In addition to the grown-up activities you enjoy now, add recreational activities from your teen and childhood years that you would still have fun doing now. Do not eliminate items from your list because you think they would be childish or silly.

_____ _____

_____ _____

_____ _____

_____ _____

Again, if your list of activities is very short, or if nothing you can think of seems like much fun, you have neglected the spunky, playful part of yourself. If your energy is chronically low, this could be a reason. Think about a playful, fun-loving child you know and notice all the energy she/he has.

Here are some activities listed by recovering Foodaholics:

build a fire in the fireplace	pick apples, berries, etc.
play in the leaves	bike
float in an innertube	roller skate
garden, tend plants	play board games
practice yoga	have a party
attend a concert	go for a walk
go to the theatre	enjoy a hobby
attend a movie	go to the zoo
go to a sporting event	stroll through a museum
go window shopping	hike
commune with nature	swim
dance	jump rope
go antiquing	play video games
make a snowperson or snow angel	swing in the park
go tobogganing/sledding	play jacks
explore the library	hopscotch
skip	paint
play tennis	play card games
canoe	ride horseback
work crossword puzzles	travel
go barefoot in the grass	engage in sexual activity
have a ticklefest	bowl
write limericks	wrestle
draw	tell riddles

Pick a couple of playful activities to do within the next two weeks. The more frequently you plan your fun, the better.

Contract: I will _____ on _____.

I will also _____ on _____.

Do put yourself first. When you do these activities, enjoy them and think about doing them often. If you let your little kid out to romp, she or he will need less food and be less inclined to eat impulsively.

NO-CAL STROKES

A stroke is a unit of recognition, either positive or negative, verbal or nonverbal. A "hello" from the grocer is positive and verbal; the smile with the greeting is positive and nonverbal. My sibling's "Gee, you look tubby" is verbal and negative. The frown accompanying it is nonverbal and negative. "I like being with you" is positive and unconditional. I don't have to perform to earn it. "I like your smile" is positive and conditional. I have to smile to earn it.

Count your sources of strokes by mapping them on the following diagram. Do it quickly and impulsively. Don't do any deep soul-searching. Simply judge where to place someone according to how you feel about that person. You can feel whether a person, group, or activity is positive or negative for you, and you can sense how close you feel. The levels are not absolute; you can do it your way.

FIGURE 12-1 My Sources of Strokes.

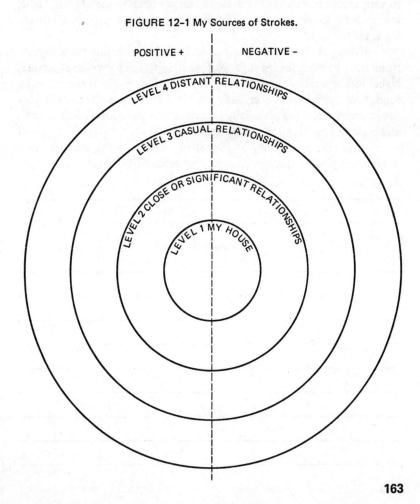

POSITIVE + | NEGATIVE –

LEVEL 4 DISTANT RELATIONSHIPS

LEVEL 3 CASUAL RELATIONSHIPS

LEVEL 2 CLOSE OR SIGNIFICANT RELATIONSHIPS

LEVEL 1 MY HOUSE

Geographical location is not an indicator of closeness or distance. For instance, Mabel, who lives in Illinois, has a friend in California and another in Montreal. She rarely sees them but feels very close to them and has warm feelings or gets lots of positive strokes when she is in contact with them or even thinks of them. On the other hand, she feels distant from her parents who are critical of her lifestyle and the person she is working hard to become. Mabel puts her friends on Level Two and her parents on Level Four. She places her cats in the most positive spot of Level One; they have an uncanny way of showing how glad they are to see her every time she walks into the room. Mabel doesn't have to do anything to earn those strokes; they're available simply because she's Mabel. Mabel wishes more people were as openly affectionate and unconditionally stroking as are her pets.

Mabel puts her bowling league on Level Two, because she always returns from bowling feeling high. Not wanting to lump everyone together, Mabel lists separately three bowling buddies of whom she is exceptionally fond. Mabel puts a co-worker, Sally, on Level Three, straddling the line between positive and negative. Sally is positive and treats Mabel well at times and is picky or prickly for no clear reason at other times.

After taking inventory of your stroke sources, think about any new awarenesses you have, or conclusions you reach. Write them here:

_____

_____

_____

_____

_____

_____

_____

_____

_____

_____

_____

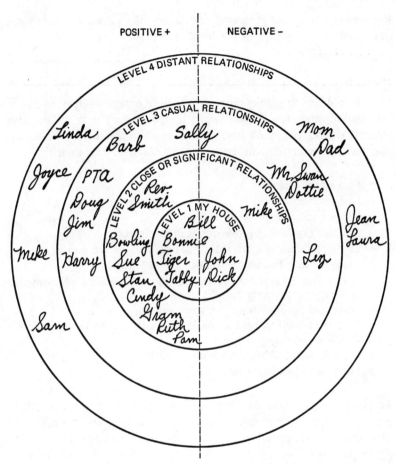

FIGURE 12-2 Mabel's Sources of Strokes.

Decide on two things you will do to get more positive strokes. Do not focus on the negative side of your chart. Turning a sow's ear into a silk purse takes considerable energy and fortitude. You may well get dozens more negative strokes when you increase your contact with negative people. Instead, note your positive sources and decide how you will capitalize on them.

Some methods to increase positive strokes are: (1) ask for strokes (they are just as valuable that way, unless you have and keep a rule that they are worth less), (2) spend more time with one or more of your positive people, (3) contact geographically distant folks via letter or telephone, or (4) make a date with a friend who is positive and fun to be with.

Contract: I will _____

and _____.

In addition to getting more strokes from outside sources, begin giving yourself more, too. Start a Stroke Journal, a diary in which you give yourself strokes you don't have to earn and also credit for your accomplishments of any magnitude. Here are some examples from journals:

- I am a neat person.
- I am lovable.
- I took good care of myself today.
- I ate healthy foods for two out of three meals.
- This binge was the shortest/least destructive I've ever had.
- I binged today for the first time in a week. I'm improving.
- I am becoming ingenious at treating myself. I bought a Snoopy cup at the supermarket instead of a snack.
- I managed the Jones's project very capably.
- I allowed myself to feel bad about being criticized today for a shorter time than usual.
- I told Ronald I didn't deserve his put-downs.
- I refused to talk about food with Michele.

To plump out your Stroke Journal instead of yourself, add the compliments you receive from others. Someday, when you are depressed and can't think of a single thing good about yourself and you are tempted to fill yourself with food, go back over the pages of your Journal and gloat over your nonfood strokes.

We have each made some decisions about what we're worth and how we deserve to be treated. Sometimes we form those ideas very early in life and base them on inadequate information. If your Stroke Inventory shows you that you have more than an occasional person in your life who treats you poorly, you may have taught them to treat you that way, or gathered these particular folks around you because you thought that was what you deserved.

In time, after you have built yourself a solid base of positive strokes, when you feel fairly confident and stable on a positive foundation, you might decide to take the next step—decreasing your negative strokes.

Which of your sources of negative strokes would you be better off avoiding completely? Are there some you can gradually retrain to treat you better? You can say to them:

- Your criticism hurts, and it is damaging our relationship.
- I don't like it when you talk to me that way.
- Stop! I do not deserve this.
- I will not listen when you berate me. I will leave the room/hang up the phone. (Then do it!)
- Your complaining really gets me down. I have decided to look at the sunny side of life. Have you heard that the Smiths found a lovely new place?
- I already have a bunch of problems. These days it is too much for me to hear yours too. How are you going to celebrate this beautiful weather?

When we use our power to stop or to avoid negative strokes, we increase our self-esteem.

RELAXATION TIME AND TECHNIQUES

It requires a fair amount of assertiveness and self-care for us to take the time to relax. The daily 20 to 40 minutes (more if we want) is a gift we give ourselves.

Salina really dreaded dinnertime at her house. Each day, she returned home from a tough and exacting job, only to encounter a frenzied mix of family problems, questions, demands, and deadlines. She felt defeated before the evening began, too tired from her day at the office to enjoy her limited time at home. Now, Salina meditates for 20 minutes before she deals with anything on the home front. Meditation facilitates the daily transition she makes from her work world to her home and family. After a short period of quiet meditation, Salina enjoys feelings of refreshment and new-found energy that carry over to enrich her evening activities. She has also discovered that what she had always identified as raging 5 o'clock hunger pangs was really tension and fatigue.

It took determination on Salina's part to convince her family that for her this 20-minute relaxation time-out was non-negotiable. They would have to learn that she would not interrupt her meditation to mediate arguments, search for the cat, or answer the telephone. After dealing with her initial feelings of guilt and distraction, Salina began to thoroughly enjoy her relaxation time. "I luxuriated in it. I often think: 'Imagine, this whole 20 minutes is mine, all mine.'"

Meditation is one technique for relaxing. There are books on how to meditate. There are meditation classes. Using a relaxation tape is another technique. For information about where to get a relaxation tape, contact local psychotherapists or human service agencies. You can also order a relaxation tape from the Foodaholics' Treatment Center.[1]

Dr. Herbert Benson's book, *The Relaxation Response*[2] contains instructions for another method of effective relaxation. In addition, concentrating on and deepening our breathing is a simple but useful method requiring no special time or place.

Actually, the effectiveness of any relaxation technique is determined only by what works for you. If you find a short nap to be delightfully refreshing, if listening to soft music or watching the clouds roll by is soothing for you—do it!

It is important to choose a fairly regular time and place to relax and to be only slightly flexible with it. A quiet, comforting spot where you will be uninterrupted is optimal, but when necessary I have meditated at my desk or in an airport.

I recommend sitting in a comfortable chair. Lying down will help you fall asleep, if that is what you intend. Allow yourself to experience this time in whatever way seems natural for you. If you feel sleepy, don't fight sleep. If your mind scurries frantically, don't push yourself to relax or decide you can't do it. Gently focus on your breathing, the word you are repeating, or a sound. Continue this process for your entire time.

Even when you would swear you are not relaxing, you will still achieve relaxation several levels deeper than when you began. If you consistently use these methods, no matter how poorly you think you are doing, you will gradually improve your ability to relax. Soon you will begin to notice the calming effect in your daily life.

PHYSICAL ACTIVITY

Physical activity need not be a grunt-and-grit-your-teeth-and-dread-it form of exercise. Put an *X* next to the activities you enjoy:

walking	jumping rope
swimming	yoga
fast dancing	aerobics
weight lifting	tai chi
softball	volleyball
boxing	trampoline
roller skating	running
bioenergetics	biking
ballet	stationary cycle
jazz-exercise	Other _____
raquetball	
tennis	_____
	_____

One of the primary benefits of any form of physical activity is a heightened sense of body awareness. In order to facilitate this awareness, pay attention to each of your sensations during the physical activity: How are you breathing? Where in your body do you feel weak or strong, tense or relaxed? How do you feel as you move different parts of your anatomy? How do your feet and legs feel as they touch the ground? Notice how you experience different surfaces such as grass, cement, or gravel. Use physical activity to sharpen awareness of your body rather than as a method of mastering a particular activity or sport.

Regular physical activity is best—three to four times a week is frequent enough to be beneficial and yet not so frequent as to encourage compulsivity. Contract with yourself for what you will do for your physical activity. (In your contract state your frequency and time of day for your selected activities. Set reasonable and attainable goals.)

I will _____

_____

_____

When embarking on a new program of running, walking, biking, or swimming, set a time goal rather than a distance goal and do not overextend yourself. Ten minutes of running is a great accomplishment when you are out of condition. You can always walk if you get tired. Twenty minutes of walking is a fine start, too. You have plenty of time in which to increase the pace or the distance.

Physical activity is also a powerful antidote for depression. For more information on treating yourself with exercise, read *The Book of Hope*, by Helen DeRosis and Victoria Pellegrino.[3]

Regular relaxation methods and physical activities will help you learn to pay attention to your body. Your body has been talking to you all along, but if you are a typical Foodaholic, you have trained yourself well to ignore it. Listen to what it tells you, and learn to trust the information you receive.

Developing a healthy eating program depends on your listening for and heeding the messages your body regularly gives you. Your program will best serve you if you experiment and make decisions about eating and exercising based on your internal sensations as well as on external information about nutrition and the undisputed value of healthy eating behavior.

NOTES

1. Foodaholics' Treatment Center, 7250 France Avenue South, Minneapolis, MN, 55435. Cost is $10.00.
2. Herbert Benson, *The Relaxation Response.* (New York: William Morrow and Company, 1975).
3. Helen A. DeRosis and Victoria Y. Pellegrino, *The Book of Hope.* (New York: Macmillan and Company, 1976).

13

Developing a Healthy Eating Program

The food plan that has worked best for me is one that I designed especially for myself. I can easily find fault with any diet or eating program. I need to customize it to my own needs and reactions. I know which foods are my binge foods or my favorites. I know how readily accessible the food should be. I know how willing I am to spend my time and energy preparing food. I have redesigned my Healthy Eating Program to reflect the increasing awareness I have of my emotional and physical responses to specific foods.

STEPS TO TAKE

You, too, will want to experiment. Take the first step now by designing your preliminary food plan. Do not expect it to be permanent or final. Changing from a destructive to a healthy eater is an ongoing, lifetime process. You can become a healthy eater gradually. It is only reasonable to expect that a profound change in both eating behavior and lifestyle takes time. You set yourself up for failure when you expect to change overnight.

Doing the following steps will help you develop your individualized Healthy Eating Program. When you finish the steps, you will have indicated lists of foods you can eat freely, those you can use to plan snacks, those foods which you must avoid, and a basic menu plan for everyday meals and special occasions.

Step 1

Make a list of foods that are taboo. This includes your binge foods, the ones you crave. Those on the list which you "hunger for" regularly and cannot seem to do without may be your clue to a food allergy. Check Foods to Avoid, pages 66–67 and write on your list any items that apply to you.

Step 2

Make a second list of foods that are non-destructive snacks or treats for you. These foods do not leave you feeling less well and do not increase your cravings. Foods such as nuts, dried fruits, exotic fruits such as mango, papaya, kiwi, pomegranate, pineapple, berries, and melon are possible snacks. So is popcorn; without grease, butter or too much salt, it is a fine nutritious snack. Popcorn is even a good item to have on hand for a planned binge.

Celeste adores popcorn, and schedules a Sunday evening pig-out! She eats it instead of dinner while watching TV. Sometimes she eats a whole dishpanful. She feels satisfied for a week or two and suffers no ill effects.

Priscilla tried Celeste's method of popcorn binging. She ate it on Sunday night and continued every night for the rest of the week. Her eating behavior went crazy. But for her it was a learning experience. She discovered that she is addicted to popcorn, canned corn, cream of corn soup, corn bread, and corn chips. Priscilla found she has an allergy to corn. As reluctant as she was to give up her favorite food, Priscilla feels relieved: "I got rid of my food obsession. I feel free and in control."

Step 3

Make a list of permissible binge foods, those that have few calories, lots of nutrients and that can be eaten in quantity. See the Free Foods list, page 175. Subtract items you find undesirable and add your own special ones.

Step 4

At this point pencil in your meal plan, using all the food types: protein, fruits, vegetables, dairy products, and grains. First, plan your daily meals. Then design an appealing meal plan for special times like weekends, parties, or vacations. You can protect yourself from overeating during those times by considering what foods might be offered and developing a strategy to keep your food intake reasonable and healthy.

From your basic meal plan you may want to develop a more detailed menu plan. Do not aim for your ideal intake too quickly. Keep a nurturing and objective view of what is reasonable and possible for you now. You can change your preliminary plan as you progress.

DARLA'S STORY

Darla took charge of her vacation eating instead of letting the available food control her. She stuck to her basic meal plan for breakfast and lunch, and still included some specialties of the region. She ate anything she wanted for dinner except for the gooey desserts that activate her binging. She contracted with herself to eat dinner slowly and pleasurably and to stop eating when she was full no matter what food remained. Darla enjoyed her vacation more than ever before. She felt indulged and yet experienced none of the guilt, bloating, and lethargy that had been part of her vacations in the past. In addition Darla received some surprise dividends: she didn't feel as if she had to drag herself back to work, and she didn't, as usual, have to diet after gaining weight on vacation.

Step 5

From your list of nondestructive treats, plan your snacks just as you do your meals. Hypoglycemics will need a snack between meals to avoid the symptoms of low blood sugar. Many people experience a low point between 3 and 5 P.M. If this is a difficult time for you, always plan to have an appropriate snack with you in the late afternoon. If your workday commonly ends with you feeling ravenous and considering a binge, stave off your crazy munchies by eating fruit and/or nuts before your hunger feels unmanageable.

A particularly good eating program is a somewhat less rigid version of the hypoglycemic diet. Junk foods are nutritionally empty calories for

TABLE 13-1
MY HEALTHY FOOD PLAN

1. *TABOO FOODS*	4. *MEAL PLAN*
	Breakfast
	Every day
2. *TREATS OR SNACK FOODS*	Special occasion
	Lunch
	Every day
3. *FREE FOODS*	Special occasion
artichokes	
asparagus	
bouillon (check for sugar and salt)	
broccoli	*Dinner*
cabbage	Every day
carrots (no more than 1 lb. daily)	
cauliflower	
celery	
cucumber	Special occasion
green pepper	
herbal tea	
jicama	
kohlrabi	5. *PLANNED SNACKS*
lettuce	a. number?
radishes	
rutabaga	b. time(s) of day?
sprouts	
zucchini	c. snack menu?
add your own:	

everybody. Use discrimination in planning whatever processed foods you must eat. Many people in the United States need less meat, fat, sugar, and salt, but more vegetables, fruit, grains, and legumes.

Designing your own eating program is an opportunity to take inventory of your likes and dislikes, and select foods that are satisfying to you as well as nutritious. You can create a food plan which you will enjoy and look forward to instead of feeling denied and deprived.

When you deviate from your food plan, do not scold or condemn yourself. It is not meant to be that rigid. Nor should you give up, thinking: "Oh well, I blew it. I might as well go whole hog." One slip does not mean you are helpless, a failure, or have lost control or decision-making power. You can choose how you will proceed at this time.

Alternative 1

You can pick yourself up and get back on your food program. A slip is your clue to the basic fallibility of human nature, not an indication of your failure or lack of character.

Alternative 2

Take a good objective look at your food program. Perhaps you have been too strict with yourself. Planning more frequent enjoyable treats might help you to avoid feelings of deprivation.

Alternative 3

Be aware of and responsible for the foods you choose and your eating behavior—even if it involves an occasional binge. Do not mindlessly stuff yourself while engrossed in a book or TV, or permit yourself randomly to devour everything in sight. Rather, decide what food you would thoroughly enjoy. Do not settle for second best. Decide exactly what you want, and then enjoy it! Say to yourself, "I like _____. I choose to eat it." Take time to experience joy in your eating. Smell and taste your food. If it interests you little after a few bites of it, or it is immediately disappointing, trust your own sensations and stop eating it.

There are two theories regarding the planning of binges. One holds that regularly spaced treats can avoid the need to binge. The other advises that we do all our binging at one time, preferably one afternoon, evening, or day per week. I suspect many of us will try both theories until we settle into the most manageable pattern for us.

A caution is in order here. People who are hypoglycemic or allergic will retard their recovery by randomly nibbling on their toxic substances. So, too, will the sugar junkie. Small, frequent doses of toxic foods cause a gradual and often imperceptible deterioration of one's health. It is better to binge all at once instead of nibbling so that feeling ill or other consequences are very clear.

Whether our deviation from our healthy eating program has been gradual and prolonged or short and intense, inevitably our memory of how well we used to feel provides the motivation to return to our healthy food program. Our slips will become shorter, less frequent, and less intense. Gradually we become addicted, in a sense, to having energy and experiencing high-level wellness. Sacrificing a few so-called goodies seems a small price to pay for our new sense of well-being.

So hide your scale and focus on turning destructive eating into healthy eating. Initially, quantity of food is less a problem than kind of food. An emphasis on weight loss may be a vehicle for sabotage. As we progress in our recovery, abstaining from addictive or destructive foods, increasing our nutritional level, and paying attention to and trusting our bodies, weight loss is usually a beneficial side effect. Whether this result is immediate or comes later is not nearly so important as experiencing and enjoying a greater degree of wellness. This path offers its own rewards, its own built-in "highs."

The following coping skills have been used by successfully recovering Foodaholics. Put a check mark next to those which would be useful for you.

Handy Household Hints

- Focus on new activities that require the use of your hands.
- Do not eat while running around or driving. Eat only while seated at a table. Treat yourself to a full-scale car wash and then make a no-eating rule for anyone in your car.
- Brush your teeth after meals. Some foods, such as red meat, leave a taste or feeling in the mouth that invites one to continue eating.
- Or, if you are lazy, carefully brush and floss after dinner. Your dread of having to do it again might prevent you from eating again before bedtime.
- Stay out of the kitchen between meals and after dinner. Plan your snacks and take them to another room.

- Do not keep other eaters company after you have finished eating.
- Tell snackers to warn you so you can be elsewhere instead of watching them eat.
- Don't keep tempting junk foods in your home. You will be doing others a favor too. If they insist on keeping their own supply of junk food, ask them to keep it out of your sight.
- Eat slowly and with pleasure to obtain more satisfaction from your food.
- When you long for a destructive food, eat your healthy meal first, and then see if you still want it.
- Know your vulnerable times, and plan something different. Change your schedule or your food plan, start a project, or engage in physical or social activity.

Handy Party Hints
- Eat before the party if you suspect that the party food available will create problems for you.
- Concentrate on the people, rather than the food.
- Inform the host of your dietary limitations so you can refuse more comfortably.
- Offer to bring your favorite healthful nutritious party food. This guarantees you some nondestructive munching.

Handy Restaurant Hints
- Know what to expect and plan what you will eat. Announce it ahead of time.
- Order à la carte to limit quantity, or plan for two meals and request a doggie bag.
- Pay attention to your body, *not your plate*. Put down your fork and stop eating when you are full.
- If the company is so stimulating that you barely taste your food, order strictly for nutritional value.
- Order something to be served immediately. Taking the edge off your appetite will keep you from devouring rolls.
- Avoid alcohol. It stimulates food cravings in sensitive individuals. Alcohol lulls both your Caretaker and your Resident Critic to sleep. There is nobody available to say "Stop eating now. Take care of yourself. Remember how you'll feel later."
- You must be assertive to take good care of yourself. You can find out if there is sugar in the onion soup, the fruit compote, or the chili, whether the fish is fresh or frozen, or if the decaffeinated coffee is instant or brewed. You can request a green vegetable instead of french fries, cottage cheese instead of creamy, sweetened cole slaw, or fish, fowl, or meat without butter or sauce.

- You can order fruit or cheese for dessert instead of feeling deprived. Again, don't be shy. If they serve strawberry pie, peach melba, or apple cobbler, they might have strawberries, apples, or peaches even if they are not on the menu. Orange-slice garnishes come from oranges and breakfast menus require grapefruit or melon.
- Don't let the comments or questions of others dissuade you. Don't try to read their minds, assuming they are scornful of your behavior. It could be that they are feeling somewhat competitive or envious about your ability to take care of yourself so well. In any event, you are not responsible for their feelings, only your own. Allow yourself to feel ingenious, decisive, and proud!
- If a vulnerable part of you feels deprived, plan a nonfood reward.

Handy Hints for Meetings or Preplanned Meals
- You may need to eat ahead.
- If the house special served at your meetings is destructive for you or heavy and full of calories, you don't have to eat it even though you have paid for it. Most hotels and restaurants are willing to provide a salad or omelet on special order. You and your health are worth the extra cost.
- Decide what you will and won't eat, and then take charge of your environment. You can have your bread and butter plate or coffee cup removed instead of having to deny repeated requests to serve you. You can request a salad without dressing or with separate dressing so you can control the amount. Refusing the dessert is easier than pretending it isn't there. For many of us, ignoring a food placed before us for the duration of the meal or the specific course is agonizing. Making the decision to not eat it *once* is difficult enough!
- Often you can call ahead to order a vegetarian meal for a meeting or when flying. Vegetarian or diabetic meals tend to be simply prepared and very nutritious.

Whenever possible, do not deny yourself healthy foods because of cost. Your junk food used to cost you dearly. Think of the good food as an investment in your health. Physical and financial dividends will accrue later in your life. The cost of out-of-season produce or other nutritious indulgences is small compared to the cost of medical bills or hospitalization. *If you don't take care of your body, where will you live?*

14

HELP Lies in the Healthy Eating and Lifestyle Program

STEPS TO RECOVERY

The 12-Step Foodaholics' Recovery Program is summarized in this chapter. It is not only a vehicle for growth and health, both emotional and physical, but a lifetime pursuit of high-level wellness. The extent to which you work your steps is the extent to which you will recover from your eating disorder.

Step 1

I will recognize the Kid part of myself and let him/her out! Because I will allow him/her to have his/her way some of the time, the little one will have less need to sneak out and eat abusively.

Step 2

I will be a Caretaker, not a Critic to the little girl or boy in me who wants to eat unhealthy foods or quantities. I will offer her/him nondestructive foods or other diversions so that my Kid need not rebel after scolding or deprivation.

Step 3

I will acknowledge and accept my feelings and needs. Feeling mad, sad, glad, scared, or hungry are part of life. I will recognize my emotions, noting where in my body I experience each. Then I will allow myself to move into and through that experience.

Step 4

I will decide what action I will take to meet my needs or express my feelings instead of using food to sedate my feelings or needs.

Step 5

I will transform my "waits" and "untils" into "nows." I will not test my patience by forever telling myself: "Not now—later," or "Wait, wait, wait." Eating can always be now, and may be if I've ignored my wants too long.

Step 6

I will plan frequent nonfood rewards and fun. My rewards will be both earned and unearned, just because I'm me. My planned rewards or goodies are a wise substitute for food treats. Fun or play will help keep me happy, healthy, energetic, and enthusiastic. These "delicious" outlets will help lessen my inclination to eat for entertainment, amusement, or fun.

Step 7

I will keep my "stroke bucket" full by making sure that my supply of compliments and touching is enough to satisfy me and give me a sense of well-being. I will do that by:

- Asking for strokes.
- Building a support system. I will make sure that my sense of self-worth and support are not based on eating or dieting. In this way, I will not have to live up to any expectations before I can get the support and strokes that I need.

- Seeking warm, fuzzy people and situations. I will avail myself of lots of stroke sources in order to lessen my need to use food and destructive eating as forms of self-stroking.

Step 8

I will count my successes—even small ones—accepting my current weight instead of giving myself food strokes. I will acknowledge the affirmations, compliments, and successes I experience in a Stroke Journal in order to have tangible evidence of my growth and change. When I feel depleted or depressed, I will read my journal entries as a way of replenishing myself.

Step 9

I will schedule regular relaxation or meditation time. I deserve this time for myself. I will be assertive and take the time. In addition to my preferred form of relaxation or meditation, I will remember that focusing on deepening my breathing is therapeutic and relaxing in itself. I will breathe deeply in order to relax and take care of myself when I feel stressed.

Step 10

I will schedule regular physical activity that I enjoy. As I engage in my chosen form of physical activity, I will turn it into a sensual experience. I will pay attention to my breathing, breathe more deeply and notice my body's sensations. I will feel my feet on the ground and my body moving. If outdoors, I will feel the wind, sun, or rain on my face.

Step 11

I will eat for pleasure or nutrition only, taking the time to really see, smell, taste, and experience my food. I will enjoy my food rather than indiscriminantly stuffing myself or eating on the run. When I am not hungry enough to find pleasure in eating, but know that I will pay a price for skipping a meal, I will take care of myself by eating a small but nourishing meal.

Step 12

I will write down my healthy eating program and the percentage of the time it is reasonable for me to maintain it for this week. I will not fret about abstaining from my binge foods forever. I will take one day at a time, except when I have to plan preventively for a party, vacation, or special occasion. I will not measure how far I am from my ultimate goal of eating perfectly. Instead, I will notice how much I have improved since last week or last month. I will not push myself to change too fast. My recovery is a lifelong process. I will allow myself to grow and develop as a healthy eater.

V

PREVENTION IS
THE BEST MEDICINE

15

How NOT to Raise
a Foodaholic

It is affirming and positive to have a strong interest in the health and well-being of our offspring, charges and students. It is important, however, that this interest not develop into an unlimited and selfless pursuit. We are, indeed, setting ourselves up as very poor models for the young people in our lives when we regularly expend our energy on behalf of others, focus on the needs of others to the exclusion of our own, and then seek food as a resource to replenish ourselves.

The rearing of a non-Foodaholic begins at the prenatal stage. To coin that old cliché, "Charity begins at home." The more experienced you are at caretaking yourself, the better position you will be in to nurture a child. (See Chapters 10 to 14.) Learning to focus on and act upon your own needs and feelings in a direct way heightens your awareness and responsiveness to others. Your sensitivity to the child's experience will be enhanced and you will be better able to separate clearly which are the child's needs and which are your own.

Taking time to take care of yourself does not need to subtract from the care you give your charges. Rather, you give them a rare and precious gift You show them, by modeling, how to get needs met and how to deal with feelings in direct and constructive ways—instead of eating.

To children, what you do has far greater effect than what you say. Children sense what you feel. They read it in the way you hold your body and in the expression on your face. They pick up the "vibes." So if they see you reach for something to eat when you are troubled, or sad, or angry, or bored, your non-verbal messages are, "Don't think—eat," and "Don't feel—eat." And your behavior is what they imitate.[1]

Imagine your child talking to you about food, eating, and how the two of you relate to each other around these issues. A newborn infant might say: "I am totally dependent, incapable of doing anything except crying to meet my own needs. I need you to let me tell you that I want or need something while I am still too young to meet my needs myself. Give me a chance to experience my own body sensation of hunger and to decide to communicate it.

"I may feel hunger, thirst, pain, discomfort, or a need for physical contact. I can develop my ability to recognize my needs and act on them if you allow me to tell you by sucking, rooting, or reaching a full lusty cry before you feed me. These are my first steps toward body awareness and becoming responsible for myself. I can find out I am effective enough to have an impact upon my environment, other people, and upon what happens to me. As I am growing up, I need you to let me use my emerging skills in order to be responsible for myself and to control myself to the extent that I am able.

"When I feel hunger and am taking my share of the responsibility and letting you know by crying, I need your prompt response so that eating or hunger does not become an emergency. If my need to eat increases and remains unmet, my state of alarm will cause me to gobble too fast and get a stomach-ache. That is also an emergency for me, and I may scramble to ease my discomfort by eating again. Or I may learn to eat too much in order to store energy and food for the next dry spell.

"When you are responding to my hunger cues, it will be best for me if you remain calm, quiet, and unhurried. If you are anxious and your movements are quick and/or jerking, I will soon feel anxious about feeding. If the nipple on the bottle has too big a hole or you feed me too fast, I may, later in my life, experience choking or gagging when I eat, or I may continue to rapidly stuff my food down.

"I also need you to think for me, to sort out what is causing my discomfort instead of automatically assuming I am crying to be fed. Nursing is for nourishment, not for keeping me quiet or entertained. When my every whimper is met with food, I learn that food is meant to handle all feelings and problems. When food becomes my principal pacifier, the stage is set for my becoming a Foodaholic.

"I am not hungry for food shortly after feeding. Maybe I hunger to be held. Maybe I have a tummy-ache or need to burp. Maybe I need my diaper changed. Perhaps I am thirsty, and a drink of water would be better than milk. Or I could be just plain cranky. Please don't pacify my crankiness with food. Instead, hold me, comfort me, and provide a quiet environment so I can rest.

"Once I have learned to suck well and have developed an interest in eating, let me decide how much I want to eat. I cannot turn my head away easily when I am tiny, and so I need you to be sensitive to other cues. I may act bored or fall asleep. As I get older, I may turn away from the nipple or bat it with my hand.

"I need you to trust my body and the sensations I have that tell me I am full. This is the first opportunity I have in life to say 'no,' to establish my own limits. Here is where I develop the 'won't power' that goes with normal eating, rather than trying later in life to manufacture enough 'will power' so as not to abuse myself or allow others to do so. If I learn that no one pays attention to my refusals, I may become someone who is handicapped in refusing food, sex, drugs, and other folks' endless demands.

"At the age of six months, I begin exploring my environment by putting everything possible in my mouth, tasting it, chewing it. You can help me explore the world of food too. I need you to decide which foods are safe—ones that cannot be broken down into small, hard particles that I could aspirate into my trachea and choke on. I need you to prepare my food so that it can be easily chewed, swallowed and held.

"I can enjoy discovering chewable foods—bread, hambones, dried squid, firm cooked vegetables, hard salami. As my gross motor coordination becomes more finely tuned, I can zero in on small things—green peas, cereal flakes, and foods like that. Eventually I will become interested in learning to use tools such as a spoon, a leaf, or chopsticks.[2] Protect my right to make a mess and don't pressure me about it. I need to experiment with food and utensils so that I can establish self-feeding skills. Even after I learn to use a spoon and fork, I will continue to enjoy hand foods.

"As I grow older, I need less milk per feeding, and my hunger occurs less frequently. By the end of the first year, I may only need a pint of milk a day. One reason is that my growth will probably slow to the point where all I need is a hearty meal every day or two with small nibbles in between. If I eat little, it still means you are doing a fine job as a parent. It isn't really your job to 'get food into' me. Your job is to provide the food and offer it to me. It is my job to get it into myself. When you get panicky and pushy, you act as if I am inept at my job of deciding when I'm hungry or full. When I refuse your very kind food offerings, it does not mean that you are inadequate, that I don't love you, or that I am refusing your love. It just means that I am not hungry.

"Sometimes I will have unusual food binges, eating odd combinations which are likely to provide, in the long run, an excellent nutritional balance. If I am not introduced to ice cream, candy, soft drinks, sugared cereal, cookies, or other sweets, I am likely to prefer unusual but healthy bings. Would you believe eight sardines in one meal at the age of eight months? How about twenty-eight boiled shrimp?[3] Or a penchant for peanut butter sandwiches, salami, and cucumbers at the age of ten months?

"When I am allowed my food jags, I will satisfy my needs, my cravings for that food, and will be interested to go on to eat other things, especially if it's not an issue with my parents.

"The best way to turn me into an undereater or an overeater is to make a point of how much I do or don't eat. When I reach the "Terrific Twos,"[4] my task is to develop some independence and separateness. The worst thing you can do is pressure me about food. As soon as you let me know that this is the most important thing to you, that's probably the first place I'll rebel. If you force foods, mealtime will become a battleground for both of us. And I have a secret—you are bigger and I need grown-ups to take care of me, so sometimes you can get real powerful and insistent and I may have to take care of you instead of doing what's right for me. I may have to 'eat the beans for Grandma' or 'join the clean plate club.' You can win the small skirmishes, but you can't win the war. I can play 'beat 'em' by dawdling with my food so mealtime takes forever, I can start spilling more, or sneaking it to the dog. I can throw up or I can get a tummy-ache. I could also play 'join 'em' by eating everything in sight in order to please you, but then you won't be happy about that behavior when I eat lots of junk or get fat.

"When you introduce new foods, don't push me beyond that first taste. It may take me a little while to grow up and like that food. We can experiment again every couple of weeks to see, for example, if I like peas.

"By the age of two or so I can begin to help with the preparation of food. I love to mix and stir and pour. I can peel a boiled egg and help set the table. When I am involved in planning, preparation, and serving of food, I have a vested interest in what is served. When I serve myself, eventually I learn to choose only as much food as I can handle.

"I can begin to help myself. If you slice the cheese or meat, I can make my own sandwich and feel very proud of doing so. By the age of three I can even manage a peanut butter and banana sandwich or other concoctions, if you will allow a little extra time and confusion. I can use this for a substitute dinner when I (yechhh!) don't want what you made. We don't have to make a big scene over this. Instead we can have some house rules that everybody respects. For example:

- At least taste everything that is served. If it is a new food, we can not know for sure that we don't like it until we try it. If the food is something commonly served in our family, we can try tasting it again every couple of weeks or so.
- No continuous complaining about food. If we don't like something after the first bite or from previous experience (yuk! liver again!), we don't have to eat it, but we won't whine or rant and rave about our don't-likes. We can eat the other foods on the table or make ourselves a different meal. We will not substitute sugary or starchy snacks.
- We can skip a meal if we want to, but snacks or the next meal will not be served any earlier. If we get hungry, we learn that hunger is a feeling we don't have to be afraid of. We can survive being hungry for a while.
- Each person has charge of his/her own meal. No one else minds the business of anyone else's plate. Comments about too much, not enough, you didn't eat, clean up your plate, are outlawed.
- Desserts are real food, not sweets. Fruit is the best dessert for us and sometimes we can have whole grain cookies or muffins sweetened with fruit. We can eat our dessert any way we want—before, after, or during a meal, or not at all. Dessert is never a reward or a bribe. It has the same priority as other foods.
- Snacks are real foods that are good for us too. They give us 1/4 to 1/3 of our nourishment. We snack on vegetables, fruits or fruit juice (not 'ade), nuts, seeds, cheese, whole grains, or combinations of these foods. Snacks are available in the middle of the morning, afternoon, and evening. We only eat at snacktime; we do not nibble all day.
- We have all our junk-food snacks at one specific time each week. Saturday morning while watching cartoons is a good time. We save

all the candy bars, lollipops, Twinkies, and other stuff that folks give us. Besides that, we can add some items to the grocery list for our junk time. We can eat whatever we want and as much as we want. Then our teeth get brushed, and we also learn what junk food feels like in our bodies. Sometimes folks notice and point out to us how we behave differently after we eat junk foods and sweets. Eventually we may become aware of it ourselves.

"You can tell me how nicely I'm growing, and point out how the nutrients in my food are helping me. I like knowing that milk gives me calcium and protein for strong teeth and bones, and green pepper and raisins have iron. Pretty soon I can decide to choose an orange for its vitamin C instead of candy which does not help me grow or have energy, but steals the nutrients from my other foods or my body. I may enthusiastically eat carrots for the vitamin A which helps people see better in the dark.

"You don't have to lecture me. I feel angry and confused when you keep telling me that I should eat my spinach ' 'cause it's good for me.' You can just talk to me matter-of-factly, and share what you know about food as we're shopping, preparing, or serving. You can say why you're hunting for a green vegetable to go with dinner. You can tell me about the wonderful whole grains in the new kind of bread we found. You can count for me all the different sugars in that cereal you just put back on the grocery shelf. You can talk about a balanced diet, and pretty soon I'll learn to balance my own. You can share your reasons for having milk instead of soft drinks, orange juice instead of powdered concentrate or orangeade, brown rice instead of white, baked potatoes instead of french fries.

"You can show me how to act on my feelings instead of sedating them with food. I need to learn that when I am troubled or angry, sad or bored, I can feel and think and act instead of turning to food. I learn from watching what you do when you are troubled, and I need you to help me discover what works best for me.

- I can talk about it and welcome your encouragement.
- I can learn to change a situation that is troubling me. I may say "I can't," but if you believe there are always options, you can help me explore alternatives and solve problems I may think are unsolvable. This is one of those skills that helps me feel powerful and self-responsible. It may enable me to cope and handle problems and my emotions when I am grown up and on my own.
- I can do something physical like walking, biking, playing tag, or exercising. Physical activity can drive the "blues" away and then we can both more easily see and try different solutions to problems.[5]

"I'm glad when you don't carry a big myth in your head that I'm supposed to be happy and pleasant all the time. I wish unpleasant feelings weren't a part of life, but that's true only in fairy tales. You teach me to be healthy and self-sufficient when you don't assume total responsibility for making and keeping me happy. This way, you don't have to haul out your magic wand and 'fix' or change my feelings into the 'right' ones. I like it when you just support and accept my negative feelings by saying things like: 'You seem to want to be sad and alone. If you want to stay in here for a while, I'll see that the others don't disturb you.' Or, 'You don't seem to be having a very good day today. Everybody has those days sometimes. Be sure to let me know if you need anything from me.'[6]

"Like most children, I can be very angry, especially when I am about two years old. I need to feel and express that emotion in safe and appropriate ways. Eating to drown out the anger is not appropriate and certainly isn't constructive. Instead, help me (and yourself, if you have forgotten how to be angry) learn to vent angry feelings by:

- Kicking a pillow or a soccer ball.
- Stomping up the stairs.
- Slamming a door (if you and the house can take it).
- Changing the situation I am angry about.
- Tearing apart an old Nerf ball.
- Hitting a punching bag or one of those inflatable figures that falls down and then pops back up again. (I think every house should have some kind of punching bag for grown-ups and kids to hit.)
- Saying to the person I'm mad at: "I don't like what you did!" I can then learn to tell people what I want them to do differently. Even if they won't do it, I have expressed my anger in a nondestructive way and I will probably feel better for having done that.[7]
- Telling those around me: "I need to grump for a few minutes. It's not your fault and you don't have to try and make me feel better." Then I can get it off my chest, particularly if my reasons for being angry don't even make sense. After all, I feel my anger in my body even when I can't figure out why I'm angry. I could mistake that feeling for hunger if I don't recognize it.

"Anger is not solved with milk and cookies, and neither is boredom. Grown-ups and children sometimes confuse hunger with boredom. I can easily initiate that confusion when I'm only a toddler. I may beg constantly for food because I don't yet know how to channel my considerable energy and need for activity. I may not have learned to play by myself yet. When

I am bored, I am searching for stimulation and strokes—someone to notice me, listen to me, talk to me, and touch me. I can eat as an activity and a way of giving myself strokes. Since eating doesn't affect my boredom, I will feel the need to eat again and again. You can show me some ways to jump off that uncomfortable merry-go-round by saying:

- Eating is to take care of feeling hungry, not bored. Let's get the blocks out and build a tower.
- I think that you really want to spend some time with me, not eat. How would it be if I build with the Legos with you for a few minutes?
- We don't have snacks until the school kids get home, but I'm so glad you came to talk with me. How are you doing?
- How about a big fat hug instead of a cookie?[8]

"I like it when you offer physical strokes—holding, touching, being close together—or toys or activities, particularly when I'm feeling antsy.

"If I have developed Foodaholic thinking, you can encourage me to straighten it out by confronting me gently and caringly:

- You just finished a big lunch half an hour ago. I don't think you need more food now. Let's play Parcheesi.
- The last time you ate two whole hot dogs you felt kind of sick. I don't want you to make yourself sick like that.
- You keep calling gum and candy 'goodies.' I think they are "baddies." They don't nourish your body and they cause tooth decay. I think hugs are yummy 'goodies.' Here, have a hug.
- Sure we can have some special foods for our party. Let's have healthy stuff that does nice things for our bodies. More important than eating, what games will we play?
- I would feel full after eating such a huge sandwich. Stop for a few minutes and pay attention to your tummy. Does it feel full?[9]

"One way you can handle it, if I am already hooked on sweets and junk foods, is to have a weekly Junk Day which is limited to an afternoon or morning. Or you can simply prohibit junk food in the house and let me complain. When you are doing something that is ultimately beneficial for me, it isn't necessary that I realize it or like it; you can do it anyway. If I am old enough to have my own money and be able to bike to the store, I can be responsible for getting my own junk food. I betcha it becomes less important when I have to pay for it and go after it. Don't feel guilty about my complaints, either. After all, drugs are bad for my body too, and you wouldn't get them for me, no matter how hard I begged, would you? Sugar is a drug and empty calories are bad for my body. They leech the nutrients I need to grow, to be calm and stable, and to think well. So you shouldn't provide me with that kind of drug either.

"We can stop hassling about my not liking school lunches or the ones you pack when I have a spot in the kitchen that is all mine for about an hour after school or after dinner. I can indulge in all sorts of brown-bag creativity, make a mess doing it, and clean up after myself. Adding some nutritional food items to the family grocery list helps me to learn menu planning, too.

"Even if I am already fat, it is not too late to establish some good practical rules in our house (pages 191-92), that exist as healthy guidelines for food use and eating behavior. The absence of high-calorie junk food from our house won't hurt you or anyone else. Those foods harm you too, even if you're thin, and when the house rules become 'no junky stuff in this house' instead of 'fat people who are bad eat nutritiously and good people who are thin can have gooey goodies,' I can feel better about myself.

"I need to know from your actions as well as your words that you like me just the way I am. I need to feel sure that you love me no less because I am chubby. Maybe I don't agree that being chubby is a problem. I can still like myself if you don't act as if there's something wrong with me. You can only keep the food supply in the house healthy, have fruit instead of sweets for dessert, and eliminate a starch at mealtimes. That needs to be a change the whole family makes or else it seems to me that you are withholding food from me 'cause I'm bad, or ugly, or unlovable.

"I need to experiment with the food and eating behaviors open to me without having you try to make me feel guilty—even when my choices represent a deviation from my food plan or seem foolish to you. The most helpful thing you can do is to make sure that I have access to accurate, objective information about the foods required for my own good nutrition and optimal health. But please leave the decisions and choices up to me.

"While I am still growing, you cannot expect me to lose weight. I can slim down just by maintaining my weight while I get taller.

"If I express feelings of being deprived of food, please don't try and talk me out of them, or tell me how great it will be when I'm thin. Instead, you can accept and understand what I'm telling you.

"Please, however bad my eating habits or my weight gets, do not try to be my warden. I may get around to coping with my destructive eating eventually. The damage that your hounding me does to our relationship is not only irreparable, but it forces me to adapt and do it your way (if I really do it up brown, I could become anorexic) or to rebel and show you that I can darn well eat what I please. And the sad fact is that I can. I can eat at school, at my friends' homes, at the movies, at parties. There is no way you can totally control my food intake.

"Your recognizing and accepting that we are two separate and different people is the greatest gift you can give me. I need your nurturing, love, and responsiveness. Equally important to me is your support for my being myself, having my own thoughts, feelings, and values."

NOTES

1. Sandra Gordon Stoltz, "How Not to Raise A Foodaholic." *Child Care Resources*, Vol. III, Issue 7, June 1979.
2. Ellen P. MacKenzie, "The Pseudo-Nurturing Parent and the American Disease." *Transactional Analysis Journal*, Vol. 10, No. 4, October 1980.
3. *Ibid.*
4. Jean Illsley Clarke, "The Terrific Twos," *Child Care Resources*, Vol. IV, Issue 7, July 1980.
5. Stoltz, "How Not to Raise."
6. *Ibid.*
7. *Ibid.*
8. *Ibid.*
9. *Ibid.*

16
Activism Versus Destructive Eating

Accepting the fact that Foodaholism is a disorder or "disease"—a widespread, destructive, personal, family, and social disease—can lead us to develop constructive "offense mechanisms." Instead of passively accepting our junk food society, instead of confusing food with love, we can work actively to change the norms in our segment of society.

For some of us, becoming more "radicalized" or taking an activist stance is an important and healing part of our recovery process. Such a stance can be a quick cure, a sure-fire alternative to playing the Victim role.

When we feel the lure of our addiction, we can substitute activism. It is a healthy alternative for several reasons. Being an activist counters the feelings of helplessness which are often an integral part of the Foodaholic personality. Voicing what we know about the destructive effects of food abuse helps us affirm our resolve not to harm ourselves by eating destructively. And the changes we effect in our environment will make a healthy regimen that much easier to maintain and tolerate. My own activism has taken various forms, usually reflecting a personal investment or interest. Several of the actions described in this chapter are well-known to me because I have taken them; other actions are based on the experience of others. While a degree of activism is necessary to initiate and maintain change, I believe it would be unhealthy for me to simply substitute an obsession with my activist role for my former obsession with food.

Following are some suggestions to guide you in becoming an advocate for healthy eating and for creating a healthy environment regarding food. You may wish to use these suggestions as they are presented, or you may prefer to adapt them, ignore them, or develop them further, just as I hope you will do with other ideas in this book.

These suggestions for influencing and changing the Foodaholic system are offered for you to consider now and choose from when you are ready to take action. If you think activists are aggressive, hard-sell people, I invite you to notice ways in which we are all activists at times. We are activists when we say to a wait-person: "A fine restaurant like this should definitely brew the decaffeinated coffee instead of serving instant." We are activists when we suggest: "For our next picnic, let's have fruit, nuts, and popcorn for munchies along with the cookies, cake, and chips."

We can take our cue from the growing number of militant non-smokers who are proclaiming their right to breathe unpolluted air. If we can't banish unhealthy foods from our environment, we can, at least, make sure that healthy ones are available as a choice.

My Foodaholic friend, Tammy, loudly bemoaned the supply of sweet foods which management offered for purchase in her work place. "I can walk past the junky stuff most of the time," she said, "but then there is a day when I oversleep and don't have time to make lunch, and I have too much work to be able to eat out. By two o'clock, I'm likely to be eating a candy bar from the office supply."

"Ask your boss to remove it," I suggested. "Offer to bring in a box of apples and oranges and bags of nuts instead."

"That wouldn't be fair," Tammy protested. "Most of the people I work with don't have a food problem. Those candy bars and cookies don't do them any harm."

I think Tammy missed the point. Instead of meekly assuming that sugar and junk foods were her personal cross to bear, she could have strongly asserted the fact that those chemically laden, nutritionally deficient snacks aren't good for *anyone*.

When Tammy did decide to speak up, she discovered unexpected support from co-workers who had also been afraid of seeming negative or "weird," but who also felt burdened by the unspoken invitations to eat destructively.

Like Tammy, we can ask to have the processed junk food supply in

our office refrigerator or snacks box eliminated, and quality whole foods substituted. While we're at it, we might request decaffeinated coffee or herb tea next to the coffee pot and/or a spring-water dispenser.

If there is a vending machine in our work or recreation area that dispenses only candy bars, fruit pies, cookies, and chips, we could call the vending machine company and ask for a selection of fruits and additive-free peanuts, almonds, raisins, and popcorn. We can ask co-workers to join us in calling the vendor and requesting healthful choices. Or we could type our request in the form of a petition and tape it to the front of the vending machine, so that other people in the building add their names to ours.

We could confront the office sweets pusher, the one with the glass jar of chocolates or jelly beans sitting on the front of his/her desk. We might tell that person that poison isn't something to be flaunted. Or we could bring a bag of fruit-and-nut mix for the next refill and tell him/her pointedly where we bought it.

Just about any place people gather, there's food—and an opportunity to do some consciousness-raising. We could call the person in charge of our after-church coffee-and-cookies hour and suggest an alternative. How about cider, cheese, and crackers? Or, consider punch (soda and unsweetened juice), fruit and nut mix, and pure corn chips. We can do the same with our PTA, singles group, condo association, bridge club, AA chapter, or professional organization.

Just when we're afraid of appearing to be pushy, we might think for a minute about how absurd it is for a group of people to get together for some constructive purpose, and then serve destructive foods after the meeting. We can remember, too, the earlier chapters in this book that analyze the mental and emotional effects of sugar addiction and food allergies. Do we really want vital group decisions affecting us made by people who are confused, sleepy or otherwise affected by their biochemical reaction to sugar, sulfur, or caffeine?

If we have contacts with children, particularly those between the ages of six and twelve, we have a wonderful opportunity for activism. We can make use of the natural curiosity of children about new ideas and their boundless energy by volunteering to give a healthy eating presentation for a school assembly or by doing a healthy eating unit with students, Girl Scouts, Boy Scouts, Camp Fire or 4-H groups.

Once we get the new information about healthy eating to the kids, we can be pretty sure that they'll spread the information to their parents and friends. In fact, I made some of my initial moves away from destructive eating because my son was encouraged to experiment with whole-foods eating by a health-conscious biology teacher. His curiosity about nutrition was contagious. After I had adopted many of my son's food changes, I then had a baking session with a Brownie Scout troop. I taught them to bake, sweetening only with unadulterated whole foods such as coconut, bananas, natural applesauce, and dates. You might say I unbrownied the Brownies!

Taking an active stance regarding our food needs is good modeling for children and grownups. It also may teach others to treat us better. Being a good caretaker to ourselves implicitly conveys a message of self-respect: "I count. I take myself and my needs seriously. I am entitled to enjoy a high level of wellness." Those who discount, minimize, or joke about our needs and feelings are less likely to do so when we treat ourselves as if we deserve better and expect them to treat us respectfully as well.

Tom told his weekend host, Jack, of his sugar sensitivity and suggested that Jack not serve baked goods or sweets on Tom's account, since he wouldn't be eating any. The food provided was delightful and all allowable on Tom's healthy eating program with the exception of a masterpiece of a cake served to a large gathering. Jack did not even offer Tom any; he already expected Tom's refusal.

Going on a vacation with an active, practicing Foodaholic was threatening to Marla. She turned the tide and actually lost weight by taking charge of her meals. She ate breakfast early and alone, planned afternoon activities immediately after lunch to avoid having time for an eating orgy, and every other evening she selected the restaurant. Marla made a contract with herself to pay careful attention to her body and to put her fork down and stop eating as soon as she experienced a feeling of fullness.

Gwen drove to visit her Foodaholic family in another city armed with a cooler of diet soda, fruit and nut snack mix, cut vegetables, and fresh fruit. When her family began to haul out their extensive supply of junk food, Gwen simply delved into her own private supply. Family members were so interested that on her next visit Gwen took enough healthy food to share with them. On the third visit, her family served the foods Gwen preferred.

Throughout this book, we've pointed out the similarities between Foodaholism and other forms of chemical dependency. Unfortunately, some people in the chemical dependency field have a blind spot about eating disorders. Les, who participated in a community chemical dependency awareness day planning committee, was horrified to hear committee members suggest setting aside a part of the budget for junk food. He quickly spoke up to say that junk food had no place in a chemical dependency seminar—and we can do the same in our groups and organizations.

If we belong to Alcoholics Anonymous, Al-Anon, or another chemical dependency support or treatment group where refreshments consist of coffee and sweets, we could explain to the refreshment committee that they are essentially substituting one drug for another, instead of helping members become addiction-free. And we can point out to them that caffeine and sugar tend to aggravate the hypoglycemia that most alcoholics already have. By offering caffeine and sugar, they may be denying recovering alcoholics the experience of good health that would make sobriety an attractive, lifelong alternative.

Most educators are well aware of the prevalence of alcohol and drug abuse among high school students. School guidance counselors may welcome a reminder that food abuse is a problem too. We might send materials and a reading list so they can familiarize themselves with the problem and provide help to students who need it. We could agree to be on a committee to help set up a voluntary support program for student Foodaholics.

Many corporations these days are providing help to employees with chemical dependency problems If we work for one of them, we could call the human resources department to request that an Overeaters Anonymous group be offered in addition to AA and Al-Anon. We can enlist the department's help in getting a salad bar and fresh fruit added to the menu in the employee cafeteria.

And if we hear about a community forum on substance abuse, we can call the organizers, not just to be certain that junk food *isn't* on the agenda, but to be certain that the issue of food abuse *is*.

We are far more likely to find whole, unadulterated foods in a health food store or co-op grocery than in a supermarket. But these specialized stores are not as discriminating as they might be. We could: take a quick inventory of the local co-op grocery or health food store, read labels, see what percentage of the foods they sell is actually healthful (probably only grains, fruits, nuts, unadulterated dairy products, and herbal teas), and target a few of the most destructive products—the ones with sugar, honey, maple, or corn syrup listed first or second on the label, or those with lots of allergens like sulfur and other preservatives. Armed with this information, we might lodge a complaint to the owner or the board of directors about how destructive their sweetened or nonnutritious wares are. We can point out the discrepancy between their avowed policy of providing healthy foods and the reality of the unhealthy foods actually available in their store(s).

Sugary, highly processed, and preserved foods are manufactured for just one reason: People buy them and manufacturers make a profit. When folks gleefully chortle about their "sweet tooth," they are confessing to nothing less than an addiction. There is little that is lighthearted or gleeful about their predicament. The real glee belongs to the business community.

According to Jane Brody, "Sugar can be the ace up a food company's sleeve. When processors want to create a market for a new product or stimulate sales on an old product, they're likely to succeed by making the products sweet or sweeter."[1]

The manufacturing and advertising of sweets and other junk food won't stop until the companies are convinced that people really want an alternative. That won't happen overnight, of course. But it won't happen at all unless we start acting now.

By paying careful attention to commericals, we can identify the ones that are in poor taste, and those that misrepresent products as healthy or nourishing for us. Be wary of those commercials that seductively entice children or adults into poor eating habits or food abuse. Note especially those commercials that perpetuate myths and stereotypes about how people should look and how they should relate to each other.

When we don't like what we see, we can write to both the manufacturer and Action Line, Direct Mail Marketing Association, 6 E. 43rd Street, New York, NY 10017. We could invite others to add their signatures to our letter or to write independently. Commercials that meet with disfavor will be changed. We do have some influence.

Think about all those coupons we've clipped for frozen cheesecake, cookie mixes, ice cream, and chips. We can keep clipping! But now, instead of redeeming the coupons, we could send them back to the manufacturer with a note that says, "I won't redeem this coupon, and I won't buy your product until you considerably reduce or eliminate the sugar (or sulfur, monsodium glutamate, or salt) in it."

We can remember our absolutely favorite, destructive binge food, the one we used to think we'd walk twenty miles through a blizzard to buy when we craved it. The next time we are in the grocery store, we might take a package of our old "fix" down from the grocery shelf and note the manufacturer's name and address. After returning the package to the shelf, we could go home and write a letter to the company's customer relations department: "I will never buy another box of Gooey Goodies for my home, my work place, or my committee meetings. I will tell my friends and co-workers how destructive Gooey Goodies are. If you want my money, manufacture a sugar-free, healthful food product instead."

We could write to the Food and Drug Administration, too, telling them that carcinogens aren't the only food additives that are destructive. We can describe what sugar, sulfur, salt, or other food additives have done to our physical and emotional health, and tell them that millions of us need government protection. We might suggest a stronger educational program urging people to limit their intake of food additives, including sulfur, salt, and sugar.

We could write to our congressional representative and senator asking how they voted on Federal price supports for the sugar industry, and telling them: "I'm anti-sugar, and I vote. I think what you're doing is equivalent to using my tax dollars to support drug pushers."

We could write to the Office of the Surgeon General demanding that products containing more than 10 percent sugar in various forms, preservatives, or other chemicals carry the label: "This product may be hazardous to your health."

Sooner or later, after we've ceased being victims and have beome activists, somebody will label us "radical" or "faddist." We can turn that intended put-down around and considering it a compliment—our initiation into a group that includes the great changemakers throughout history. We could tell our accusers, "If we were meant to subsist on refined carbohydrates, we would each have a cast-iron pancreas. If we were meant to sustain ourselves on non-nutritive processed food (up to 50 percent of our supermarket space), life-affecting conditions such as obesity, diabetes, and hypoglycemia would not be on an upward trend in our society.

We need to remember that most of the people we talk to about healthy eating have the same defense mechanisms we once had. They're just as likely as we were to rationalize, joke, minimize, or lie about their food abuse. Like the rest of us, they'll need some time to let go of their defenses.

Attempting to "work someone else's program" leads to frustration for us and probably resentment and rebellion for the food addict. We can share our experiences and information as an expression of caring and to solidify our own new-found healthy patterns. After that, it is best we let go of responsibility for solving their problems so we can avoid playing psychological games.

Others' changed attitudes may surprise us. The child who says, "Don't lecture," when we talk about the evils of sugar and junk food will be overheard later giving the same lecture to his friends. Or the friend who reacts, "You've gone overboard on this healthy eating kick," will serve vegetables and fruit at the next gathering. Or the spouse who used to suggest stopping for a milkshake will suggest going for a walk instead.

When the breakthrough comes, we may be tempted to say, "I told you so." I hope we don't. I hope we just smile and say, "Thanks."

From all of us.

NOTES

1. Jane E. Brody, *Jane Brody's Nutrition Book.* (New York: W.W. Norton and Company, 1981), p. 131.

Appendixes

APPENDIX A: DIAGNOSIS

"Sophisticated interpretation of the six-hour glucose tolerance test can provide information as to the status of the glands which regulate blood sugar levels. It is a valuable diagnostic tool and should be a routine testing procedure."[1]

The Glucose Tolerance Test recommended by the Adrenal Metabolic Research Society of the Hypoglycemic Foundation (AMRS) is a five- or-six-hour, seven-sample test administered after a twelve-hour night-time fast. Your doctor or medical technician will take a fasting sample of blood, then have you drink a sugar solution. Samples of blood are taken after a half hour, an hour, and each hour thereafter for five or six hours.[2] The Foodaholics' Treatment Center also recommends a three-and-a-half hour sample. We find that many of our clients experience their lowest blood sugar reading at that time.

Glucose Tolerance Tests are usually given in the morning, but the AMRS is finding special value in afternoon testing done four or five hours after a normal breakfast and normal morning activities. The afternoon test can be used when a morning test is borderline or as a follow-up after a period of treatment.[3]

For most people, undergoing the GTT on an outpatient basis is fine. But if you have a history of seizures, convulsions, episodes of unconsciousness, or suicidal thoughts when you use sugar, hospitalization for the test is indicated.

No tobacco, food, or drink is allowed during the test. Normal, nonstrenuous physical activity, such as reading, needlework, and talking is fine. If you've found that your hypoglycemic symptoms appear or are aggravated by physical activity or stressful situations, you may want to ask your physician to combine the GTT with a stress test.

During the test, keep a record of your reactions. The sample record, Table A-1, page 207 is used by several Minneapolis agencies. Simply note any physical or emotional symptoms you experience in the column under or between specific blood samples. Use your own descriptive words; the words at the left margin are merely for your guidance.

Figure A-1 shows the results of a normal Glucose Tolerance Test[4] The numbers across the top of the chart indicate the hours when blood samples are taken. The numbers along the side of the chart show milligrams percent of blood sugar. According to the AMRS guidelines, "blood

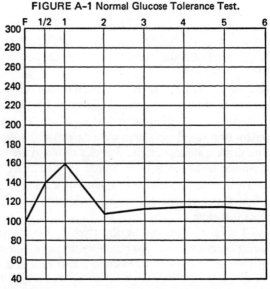

FIGURE A-1 Normal Glucose Tolerance Test.

TABLE A–1
MONITORING SYMPTOMS DURING THE GLUCOSE TOLERANCE TEST

Name _____   Date _____

		FASTING	30 MIN	1 HOUR	2 HOUR	3 HOUR	4 HOUR	5 HOUR	6 HOUR
Headache	1								
Dizzy	2								
Faint	3								
Nausea	4								
Tired	5								
Hungry	6								
Can't Concentrate	7								
Memory	8								
Vision	9								
Restless	10								
"Hung-over"	11								
Drink	12								
"Sluggish"	13								
Shaky	14								
Anxious	15								
Sweaty	16								
_____	17								
_____	18								

sugar levels should range at fasting between 80–110 milligrams percent and should rise during the next hour to 140–160 milligrams percent and return to fasting level by the second hour and *remain at that level* for the duration of the test. *Any variation from this pattern should be considered 'abnormal' and deserving of investigation.*[5]

Figure A-2 shows the normal curve in contrast to some common abnormal tests. Line A is a diabetic reaction; B through F are all types of hypoglycemic reactions. Some physicians do not diagnose hypoglycemia unless the blood sugar level falls to 60 milligrams percent, or even 50 or

FIGURE A-2 Abnormal Glucose Tolerance Tests.

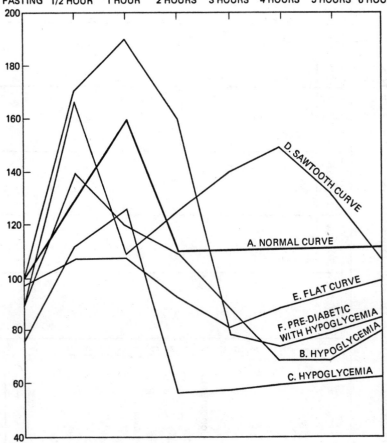

40, even if the patient is having hypoglycemic symptoms.[6] In contrast, Dr. Harvey Ross diagnoses hypoglycemia "if the blood sugar on any of the samples is more than 20 milligrams percent below the fasting level, or falls more than 50 milligrams percent in one hour, and these changes are accompanied by symptoms of hypoglycemia. . . ."[7] Other abnormal curves qualifying as indicators of hypoglycemia are the flat curve (line E on Figure A-2), which is the "failure of the blood sugar to rise 50 percent above the fasting specimen during the first hour," and the saw-tooth curve (D), which is a "marked rise of the blood sugar after the return to the fasting specimen level at the second hour."[8] The point at which the blood sugar level again rises has been called a "state of emergency." The increase indicates the body is responding to correct the abnormality.[9]

Because so many physicians don't understand or don't believe in the existence or importance of hypoglycemia, you may need to take charge. Do not settle for a fasting blood sample or a two- or- three-hour GTT. And ask for a copy of the test results rather than accepting a blanket, "Don't worry, you don't have it." As the AMRS states, "Whenever the sugar-regulating machinery reacts to the low level by producing symptoms is the point at which the individual shows hypoglycemic reaction. *No arbitrary figures have significance.*"[10] (Emphasis mine.)

The Huxley Institute for Biosocial Research, 1114 First Avenue, New York, New York 10021, will supply a list of orthomolecular physicians who will conduct allergy and Glucose Tolerance Tests.

APPENDIX B

Fasting and the reintroduction of foods is a common and reliable allergy test method. The book, *Dr. Mandell's 5-Day Allergy Relief System,*[1] details one such process, which involves a spring water fast and the separate testing of 21 foods on a preliminary diet. If complete fasting isn't practical (or bearable) Robert Eagle, the author of *Eating and Allergy*, suggests a one-week diet of lamb and pears before beginning deliberate food testing. These are two substances that very few people are allergic to.[2]

The Coca Pulse Test, devised in the 1930's by Dr. Arthur Coca, is based on evidence that the pulse rate tends to go up (or down) markedly after exposure to allergens. For three days before testing you *must* (1) stop smoking; (2) keep a written record of your pulse rate just before getting out of bed, just before each meal, three times after each meal (at half-hour intervals), and just before going to sleep; (3) write down everything you eat for three days; (4) treat any snack as a separate meal, record it, and take your pulse once before and three times after you eat it.[3]

Use your three-day record to determine your pulse differential, the difference between your highest and lowest daily reading. A differential of more than 12 shows a possible allergy. A differential of more than 16 makes it probable.

After the three-day test, record your pulse, then eat a small amount of a different food every hour. Take your pulse right before and a half-hour after you eat. If your pulse rate increases, wait until it returns to normal before you test the next food. Any food that makes your pulse increase six beats or more is probably an allergen.[4]

Kinesiologic testing may sound incredible, but it works! Extensive and reliable testing is best done by a chiropractor who has studied applied kinesiology, but you can obtain preliminary results with the procedure. You will need a friend to help you. Hold your arm straight out from your body, to the front or the side. Your tester will grasp your arm and push down firmly, but without jerking, while you try to resist. This is not an arm wrestling contest; your tester will simply be getting the "feel" of normal muscle tone. With a small amount of a specific food or beverage on your tongue, repeat the above procedure. If your arm muscles are still strong, the food is probably not an allergen. If your muscles weaken, the food most likely is an allergen.

Start with the food you suspect, or with some common allergens: wheat, corn, milk, sugar, and coffee. Don't swallow any of the foods; spit them out and rinse your mouth with water to clear the residue. You can test several foods in quick succession with this method.

If you wish to consult with an applied kinesiologist in your area, write Dr. George Goodheart, 542 Michigan Building, Detroit, Michigan 48226 for a list of qualified practitioners.

NOTES

Appendix A

1. *Hypoglycemia and Me?* (Troy, NY: Adrenal Metabolic Research Society of the Hypoglycemia Foundation, Inc., 1973), p. 10.
2. *Ibid.*, p. 5.
3. *Ibid.*, p. 9

4. *Hypoglycemia and Me?*, p. 10.
5. *Ibid.*
6. *Ibid.*, p. 8.
7. Harvey M. Ross, "Hypoglycemia," *Journal of Orthomolecular Psychiatry*, Vol. 3, No. 4, 1974.
8. *Ibid.*
9. *Hypoglycemia and Me?*, p. 8.
10. *Ibid.*

Appendix B

1. Dr. Marshall Mandell and Lynne Waller Scanlon, *Dr. Mandell's 5-Day Allergy Relief System* (New York: Thomas Y. Crowell Company, 1979), pp. 251–273.
2. Robert Eagle, *Eating and Allergy* (Garden City, NY: Doubleday and Company, 1981).
3. Dr. Arthur Coca, *The Pulse Test: Easy Allergy Detection* (New York: Arco Publishing Company, Third Edition, 1977), pp. 33–50.
4. *Ibid.*

Index

Infants, 81–83, 188–89
Insulin, 46–48
Intellectualizing, 18

Kamerman, Jack, 99
Karpman, Stephen, 143
Kinesiologic testing, 73, 210
Kunin, Richard, 46–47, 48, 96

Laugh It Off (Noland), 33
Lederer, William, 49–50
Lee, Carlton, 75
Love, food as expression of, 83–85, 94
Low blood sugar (*see* Hypoglycemia)
Low Blood Sugar and You (Fredericks), 65
Loyalty, 120–22

Mackarness, Richard, 74
Magical thinking, 96–97
Malnutrition, sugar and, 48
Mandell, Marshall, 75
Marshmallow Caretaker, 133–34
McBride, Angela Barron, 126
Media, 93–100
Meditation, 167–68, 182
Meetings, 179
Meganutrition (Kunin), 46–47, 96
Meir, Golda, 125
Migraines, 21, 53
Millman, Marcia, 99
Minerals, 68
Minuchin, Salvador, 110

Narcotics, 68
National Association of Anorexia and Associated Disorders (ANAD), 111
Negative feedback, 34
Negative strokes, 166–67
Nicotine, 68
Nittler, Alan H., 55
"No," 149–53
Noland, Jane, 33
"Nows," 159–60, 181

Obesity, sugar and, 48
Obsession, The: Reflection on The Tyranny of Slenderness (Chernin), 98
Office of the Surgeon General, 203
Orthomolecular Nutrition (Hoffer), 56

Pancreas, 46–48
Parry, Kate, 97
Party hints, 178
Passwater, Richard, 49
Peele, Stanton, 47
Pellegrino, Victoria, 170
Persecutor role, 143–47, 150
Physical activity, 162, 169–70, 182, 192
Placating, 119–20
Pleasing, 119–20
Pleasure, 156–57
Popcorn, 173
Positive strokes, 162–67
Power, 125–26
Preoccupation with food, 10–11
Principle of Accountability, 150
Protection, 123–25

Randolph, Theron, 74, 75–76
Rationalization, 17
Rebellion, 122–23
Recreational activities, 161–62, 182
Relaxation, 136–39, 167–69, 182
Relaxation Response, The (Benson), 168
Request for a Statement of Needs, 150–51
Rescuer role, 143–47, 150–51
Resident critic, 85–86, 134–36, 156
Restaurant hints, 178–79
Reuben, David, 41
Rewards, 160–61
Rigidity, 16, 25
Rinkel, Herbert J., 75
Roosevelt, Eleanor, 125
Ross, Harvey M., 56, 57, 68, 69, 209
Rotary Diversified (RD) Diet, 75–76

Sadness, 153
Salt, 95, 203
Saunders, Jeraldine, 56, 57
Saying no, 149–53
Scapegoats, 120
Selective Neglect, 150
Self Esteem: A Family Affair (Clarke), 133
Selfishness, 149
Self-ridicule, 17–18
Sexual feelings, 123–24, 155
Slenderness, ideal of, 93–94, 98–100
Smith, Robert T., 94–95
Snacks, 13–14, 174, 175, 191–92, 194
Stitt, Paul, 95